Tools for Teaching the History of Civil Rights in Milwaukee and the Nation

Edited by Michael Edmonds

Library-Archives Division

Wisconsin Historical Society

Contents

4   List of Lesson Plans

6   A Brief Summary of Milwaukee's Civil Rights Movement

7   PART ONE: Lessons about Milwaukee's Civil Rights Movement

49   PART TWO: Lessons about the Civil Rights Movement in the South

81   PART THREE: Lessons about Pivotal Events and Issues in Civil Rights History

113   Correlation of Lessons with Professional Standards

Preface

We created this book to help you teach middle and high school students about one of our nation's most dynamic social movements, the history of the Civil Rights Movement in Milwaukee and the South.

Each of its 20 lesson plans contains a page of background, facsimiles of two or three historical documents, and a page of activities connected to each document. The documents include videos, newspaper articles, maps, letters, cartoons, survey comments, photographs, fliers, diary entries, logos, advertisements, oral history interviews, statistical tables, speeches, and more.

Each document can be copied back-to-back with suggested activities (except for video and audio clips, which you will need to watch or listen to online). A table at the end correlates each lesson plan with widely accepted academic standards.

Copy and use anything that works for you. Ignore everything else. Download individual lessons in Microsoft Word at www.wisconsinhistory.org and edit them to work in your unique situation.

We've taken most of the documents from the UW-Milwaukee's March on Milwaukee digital collection (http://wihist.org/1uC7eWx) or the Wisconsin Historical Society's Freedom Summer online archive (http://wihist.org/1v0b5mh). Thousands of other historical documents are available at those two sites. National History Day contestants and AP students might want to go there to conduct deeper research on their own.

The lesson plans were written by staff of the Wisconsin Historical Society's Freedom Summer project: Michael Edmonds, Russ Faulkner, Mary Kate Kwasnik, Lotus Norton-Wisla, Kathryn Sheriff, Samantha Snyder, and Emily Swenson. The classroom activities are intended to foster critical thinking.

The Jane Bradley Pettit Foundation, the Herzfeld Foundation, the Northwestern Mutual Foundation, C. G. Schmidt, and the Weyco Charitable Trust provided funding to create and distribute this handbook. We're grateful for criticism and suggestions provided by Jasmine Alinder, Matt Blessing, Kathy Borkowski, Linda D'Aquisto, Michael Doylen, Sarah Fallon, Michael Gordon, Kurt Griesemer, Maggie Holtgrieve, Ryan Hurley, Meghan Kobs, Jennifer Koss, and Phyllis Santacroce.

The Wisconsin Historical Society has a free traveling exhibit about 1964's Mississippi Freedom Summer campaign available for secondary schools. You can see it at www.fsxbt.tumblr.com. Contact michael.edmonds@wisconsinhistory.org if you'd like to install it in your school.

Please send questions, comments, and requests for more copies to Michael Edmonds, deputy director of the Library-Archives Division at the Wisconsin Historical Society, at michael.edmonds@wisconsinhistory.org.

Best wishes for continuing success in the important work that you do.

Michael Edmonds
Deputy Director, Library-Archives
Wisconsin Historical Society

List of Lesson Plans

PART ONE
Lessons about Milwaukee's Civil Rights Movement

1. **Housing Segregation in Milwaukee in the 1960s.** Students examine a map, a statistical table, and a video clip of Father James Groppi to understand the origin of segregated neighborhoods and why fair housing became an important issue.

2. **School Segregation in Milwaukee in the 1960s.** Students investigate survey responses by Black residents and a school boycott flier to learn about segregated schools. They will compare conditions then with their own schools today.

3. **Milwaukee School Boycott, May 10, 1964.** Students analyze a political flier and a video clip, decipher their main messages, and try to imagine what they would do in similar circumstances today.

4. **Marching Across the 16th Street Bridge.** Students begin to understand the fair housing marches of 1967-68, imagine the motivations of participants, and investigate what fair housing means.

5. **How Young People Made a Difference in Milwaukee.** Students learn about teenagers' participation in Milwaukee's civil rights struggle by examining a NAACP Youth Council press release and listening to an interview with a woman who marched during the years 1963–68, when she was a high school student, .

6. **Vel Phillips and the Struggle for Fair Housing.** Students watch a four-minute video of the Milwaukee Common Council postponing action on Alderwoman Vel Phillips's proposed fair housing ordinance, analyze key provisions of the Fair Housing Act of 1968, and debate the conflict between property rights and civil rights.

7. **Busing in Milwaukee Schools since 1979.** Students examine arguments for and against busing by watching a ten-minute video, comparing Milwaukee's experience with that of Charlotte-Mecklenburg, N.C., and analyzing two 1983 letters to the editor.

8. **Segregation in Milwaukee Today.** Students discover the effects of de facto segregation by examining maps that show race and income distribution. Using the Anti-Defamation League's "Pyramid of Hate," they identify prejudice in their own lives and imagine steps they can take to change it.

PART TWO
Lessons about the Civil Rights Movement in the South

9. **Segregation in Mississippi in 1960.** Students extract information from a map, a statistical table, and a photograph; synthesize their findings; and reach conclusions about the effects of government-sponsored segregation.

10. **Segregated Schools: Winners and Losers.** Students compare school segregation in Milwaukee and Mississippi during the 1960s, consider the relationship between knowledge and power, and reflect upon the value of education in their own lives.

11. **Civil Rights: For or Against?** Students learn how to identify the main point in an informational text, assess the evidence and reasoning behind it, and decide whether to accept or reject it by analyzing a Student Nonviolent Coordinating Committee (SNCC) pamphlet and a Citizen's Council advertisement.

12. **Neutrality or Engagement?** Students investigate a political cartoon and a diary entry that highlight risks taken by civil rights workers in the 1960s. They imagine themselves in similar situations and consider conflicts, motivations, and responsibilities. Then they evaluate how much they would sacrifice for an ideal.

13. **The Power of Freedom Schools.** Students compare conflicting 1964 textbook excerpts about Black history, analyze a photograph, and draw conclusions about the value of good schools.

14. **Getting the Message Out.** Students learn how SNCC managed the media during the Civil Rights Movement, examine marketing and public relations techniques, examine their own media consumption, and write a press release.

PART THREE
Lessons about Pivotal Events and Issues in Civil Rights History.

15. *Brown v. Board of Education.* Students learn about the pivotal 1954 *Brown v. Board of Education* Supreme Court ruling by watching a PBS video, reading excerpts from the decision, and analyzing a political cartoon. They debate the proper role of government in community affairs and citizens' lives.

16. **Civil Rights Act of 1964.** By rephrasing two paragraphs from the act and analyzing a photo and an advertisement, students learn about its main provisions and why those were controversial in 1964. Activities challenge them to take a side in the conflict between civil rights and property rights and explain their stance.

17. **Voting Rights Act of 1965.** By analyzing first-person accounts from Mississippi, students discover why the act was needed and learn how literacy tests, harassment, and violence disenfranchised Black residents. Then they analyze key provisions of the act and examine challenges to voting rights in the United States today.

18. **Rights In Conflict.** Students gain a greater understanding of the relations between federal authority, local control, property rights, and civil rights, and clarify their beliefs about the role of government.

19. **Inventing Common Sense.** Students examine a 1964 *New York Times* article quoting white Mississippi residents on race relations, compare Black residents' responses, and dissect an argument about the power of the media. Then they analyze their own media consumption.

20. **Civil Disobedience.** A classroom activity that separates students by physical characteristics simulates an injustice, which students discuss in light of an excerpt from Martin Luther King's "Letter from a Birmingham Jail" and two segregationist documents. They are challenged to decide what makes a law just or unjust, what makes an action good or bad, and when civil disobedience is acceptable.

A Brief Summary of Milwaukee's Civil Rights Movement

African Americans in Milwaukee were fighting for their rights long before the movement attracted headlines in the 1960s. In 1866, for example, Ezekiel Gillespie successfully sued for the right to vote and in 1889 Black leaders organized a statewide convention that demanded an end to segregation.

The movement gained momentum with large-scale migration of Black citizens to Milwaukee after World War II. Between 1940 and 1960, Wisconsin's African American population increased by more than 500 percent, from 12,000 in 1940 to 75,000 in 1960. Most of these new residents came from Mississippi, Arkansas, and Tennessee.

For decades, city officials, bankers, realtors, and landlords had restricted African Americans to one small neighborhood on Milwaukee's near north side. As the number of residents expanded rapidly in the 1950s, population density rose to five times the average in other neighborhoods. Overcrowding, unemployment, and poverty were the inevitable consequences.

Segregated neighborhoods produced segregated schools. Despite the 1954 *Brown v. Board of Education* decision declaring segregated schools illegal, a 1960 survey found that schools in the central city were 90 percent Black. In March 1964, community activists, including attorney Lloyd Barbee, Milwaukee Common Council member Vel Phillips, and Father James Groppi, a white Catholic priest, created an organization called the Milwaukee United School Integration Committee (MUSIC). In May 1964, MUSIC organized a boycott of predominantly Black schools; more than half of Milwaukee's African American students participated.

In 1965, when Milwaukee's school board still refused to comply with B*rown v. Board*, Barbee filed a lawsuit charging the board with intentional discrimination. The city fought the lawsuit for 14 years, all the way to the U.S. Supreme Court, which ruled in Barbee's favor in March 1979. After resisting *Brown v. Board* for 25 years, Milwaukee finally began implementing a desegregation plan. It relied on redistricting, specialty (magnet) schools, and busing to eliminate all-white and all-Black schools. More than 80 percent of the students who bused to new schools were African American.

City leaders fought equally hard to maintain segregated housing. In 1962, Vel Phillips introduced an ordinance in the Common Council guaranteeing fair housing; hers was the only vote in favor of it. This happened three more times over the next six years as city officials refused to integrate neighborhoods.

In August 1967, the NAACP Youth Council and Groppi marched with 250 demonstrators to a predominantly white neighborhood to protest the Common Council's latest rejection of fair housing. Thousands of white residents greeted them, shouting obscenities and throwing rocks and bottles. Groppi became a catalyst in the fight for civil rights in Milwaukee, leading frequent demonstrations. Daily marches continued throughout the winter of 1967-68.

After Congress passed the Fair Housing Act (part of the Civil Right Act of 1968), the Milwaukee Common Council finally approved a fair housing ordinance for the city. As neighborhoods opened up to African Americans, thousands of white residents left the city: in 1960, Milwaukee had 668,000 white residents, but in 2000, it had only 298,000. Although segregation has been illegal in housing, schools, employment, and other areas of American life for nearly half a century, Milwaukee remains one of the most segregated cities in the nation today.

PART ONE

Lessons about Milwaukee's Civil Rights Movement

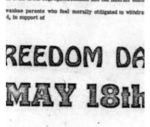 

Housing Segregation in Milwaukee in the 1950s and 1960s

Goals

Students examine a map, a statistical table, and a video clip of Father James Groppi to understand the origins of segregated neighborhoods and why fair housing became an important community issue.

Central Questions

Where did neighborhood segregation come from? Why was fair housing such an important issue?

Background Information

Until the 1960s, discriminatory laws and lending practices forced nearly all African Americans to live in a single neighborhood just north and northwest of downtown. Ninety percent of Milwaukee's subdivisions had been laid out with covenants prohibiting the sale of property to people of color, and informal agreements among realtors, lenders, and landlords reinforced those restrictions. These practices were not considered illegal until 1968; many, if not most, US cities were similarly segregated.

Black residents who tried to move out of the central city faced landlords who refused to rent to them or banks that wouldn't write mortgages. Landlords told African Americans seeking housing that vacant apartments had suddenly been rented to others, or prices and rents were much higher than had been publicly advertised.

In 1962, alderwoman Vel Phillips introduced the first ordinance in the Milwaukee Common Council to reverse this sort of discrimination. The ordinance was defeated 18-1, her vote being the only one in favor. Similar votes occurred three more times over the next six years. Finally, in 1967 and 1968, Milwaukee's NAACP Youth Council picketed the homes of alders and marched for 200 consecutive nights to demand a fair housing law. After the assasination of Martin Luther King Jr., Congress passed a national fair housing law. On April 30, 1968, the Milwaukee Common Council followed with its own ordinance. See the lesson plan, "Segregation in Milwaukee Today," (page 43) for related content.

Documents Used in This Lesson:

1. Map of Milwaukee's Black neighborhood, 1940, from "Milwaukee's Negro Community." Citizens' Governmental Research Bureau. (Milwaukee: The Bureau, 1946): page 2.
   http://wihist.org/11r0hkh
2. News clip of Father James Groppi summarizing the fight for open housing, September 20, 1967. Six minutes long. This is raw footage, abruptly edited in places.
   http://wihist.org/1zSvSXW

1. Map of Milwaukee's Black neighborhood, 1940, from "Milwaukee's Negro Community," Citizens' Governmental Research Bureau, 1946.
http://wihist.org/11r0hkh

Race Restrictive Covenants

Mr. George Brawley, a Milwaukee attorney, has recently completed a study of the race restrictive covenants contained in plats filed with the

Register of Deeds office of Milwaukee County. He estimates that 90% of subdivisions which have been platted in the City of Milwaukee since 1910 contain some type of covenant which has the effect of prohibiting the sale of the property to Negroes.

He states that in other parts of the city there are "gentlemen's agreements" not to sell or rent property to Negroes except within the area bounded by W. North, W. Juneau, N. 3rd, and N. 12th Streets.

Covenant: a legal rule
Plat: the official map of a neighborhood
Subdivision: neighborhood
Gentlemen's Agreement: promise within a private group to work together to achieve a goal

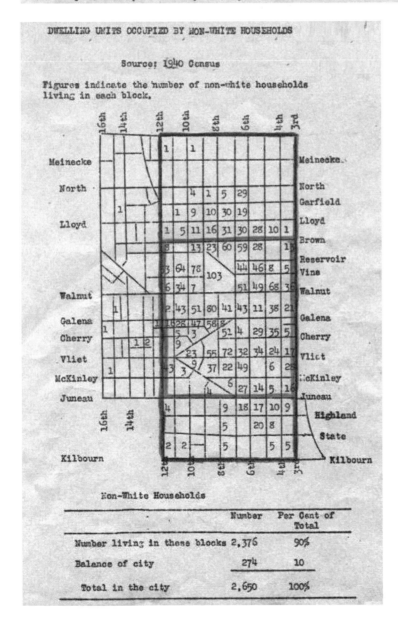

DWELLING UNITS OCCUPIED BY NON-WHITE HOUSEHOLDS

Source: 1940 Census

Figures indicate the number of non-white households living in each block.

Non-White Households

	Number	Per Cent of Total
Number living in these blocks	2,376	90%
Balance of city	274	10
Total in the city	2,650	100%

Questions

Document 1: Map of Milwaukee's Black neighborhood, 1940.

With a partner, answer these questions.

1. Look at the map closely. Can you find where I-94 is today, or I-43, or Marquette University, or the Bradley Center, or the Milwaukee Public Museum?

2. What percent of the nonwhite (African American) households in Milwaukee lived in this neighborhood? (Hint: look at the table below the map)

Document 2: News clip of Father James Groppi talking about fair housing on Sept. 20, 1967.
http://wihist.org/1zSvSXW

Questions

Document 2: News clip of Father James Groppi, Sept. 20, 1967.

Watch the six-minute video clip of Father Groppi and discuss the following questions in small groups. (Because the film is unedited raw footage, it skips around a little, especially in the second half.)

1. How does Father Groppi explain the necessity of holding marches and demonstrations in Milwaukee?

2. What happened when the small group of demonstrators reached the all-white neighborhood near South 10th and Lincoln?

3. How did construction of the freeways and urban renewal projects affect 1,000 Black families in the central city?

4. Why does Father Groppi bring up police dogs at the end of the film clip? How is his proposed response to dogs different from that of other civil rights protesters? Do you agree or disagree with what he says about nonviolence?

School Segregation in Milwaukee in the 1960s

Goals

Investigate survey responses by Black residents and a school boycott flier to learn about segregated schools. They will compare conditions then with their own schools today.

Central Questions

What were schools in Milwaukee like in the early 1960s? What were the major issues facing students and teachers? Do you see any of these issues in your own school? What can be done to improve schools and learning?

Background Information

Despite the 1954 *Brown v. Board* decision declaring racial segregation illegal, a 1960 survey of Milwaukee schools found that schools in the central city were 90 percent black. In March 1964, community activists, including attorney Lloyd Barbee, Milwaukee Common Council member Vel Phillips, and Father James Groppi organized the Milwaukee United School Integration Committee (MUSIC). In May 1964, MUSIC organized a boycott of predominantly Black schools in which more than half of African American students participated. They also challenged segregated schools through picketing, demonstrations, and other direct actions.

Parents were upset by the vast differences in quality between majority Black and majority white schools. Another point of contention was "intact busing," or transporting African American students to all-white schools but keeping them in segregated classrooms, cafeterias, and activities in those schools. Many Black children were also tracked into vocational classes instead of business or college prep classes.

In 1965, Barbee filed a lawsuit charging the Milwaukee School Board with practicing discrimination. The city fought the lawsuit for 14 years, all the way to the US Supreme Court, which finally ruled in Barbee's favor in March 1979.

Documents Used in This Lesson:

1. Comments by Black residents from *Attitude Study among Negro and White Residents in the Milwaukee Negro Residential Areas* (Milwaukee: Bisbing Business Research, 1965): 67-70.
    http://wihist.org/1uUxFM6

2. Flier recruiting residents for a march protesting segregated schools on August 28 (probably 1967) Milwaukee United School Integration Committee Records, 1964-1966, Box 1, Folder 5.
    http://wihist.org/1zVODdf

This lesson plan could be used in conjunction with Lesson 3, Milwaukee School Boycott, May 18, 1964 (p. 18) or Lesson 9, School Segregation in Mississippi in 1960 (p. 50).

Document 1: Comments by Black residents from the 1965 *Attitude Study among Negro and White Residents in the Milwaukee Negro Residential Areas.* http://wihist.org/1uUxFM6

-- Those schools should have been torn down long ago. I work
   on construction, help build schools -- in other areas they
   have everything. The lobbys are bigger than the auditoriums
   around here.

-- The curriculum is not up to date. The textbooks are not what
   they should be, and the teachers are not in sympathy with
   the kids.

-- There is so much difference between the Negro and White
   school children. Kids on the side don't know anything about
   their subjects; the way they conduct themselves and their
   environments are different. I was really suprised -- the
   the kids from this side have to play by themselves.

-- Most of the White schools have first-class facilities whereas,
   we have to use the things that they don't want anymore.

-- Because they could have lunch rooms and more playground
   space, more room on the sidewalk and more crossing guards.

-- Some of the teachers are prejudiced.

-- Well, I could say that the teachers are not rough enough on
   the kids.

-- I feel that Negro children being moved from one area to
   another is bad. It is unfair to go somewhere where you are
   not wanted. I also feel that they should have more schools
   built in Negro neighborhoods and all this trouble could
   be avoided.

-- Some kids don't get the books that they need. They get the
   old books from the White schools. I think they should
   have just what the White schools should have.

Questions

Document 1: Comments by Black residents on Milwaukee's segregated schools in 1965.

1. With two or three classmates, make a list in your own words of the problems in the schools. Does your own school have any of these problems today?

2. Decide as a group which problem was the most serious. Why did you choose that one? How do you think that problem affected students' abilities to achieve success in the future? How are these problems connected to the social and economic disparities in Milwaukee?

3. Imagine that the schools fixed all these problems and schools in Black neighborhoods were just as good as the ones in white neighborhoods. Decide if it would still be OK for Black kids and white kids to attend separate schools. Why or why not?

4. Find another group that answered question 2 or 3 differently than your group did. Ask them why, listen to their explanation, and then try to persuade them to agree with you instead.

Document 2: Flier recruiting residents for a march protesting segregated schools.
http://wihist.org/1zVODdf

How much is Milwaukee segregation costing YOU and ME?

INFERIOR SCHOOLS

"One of the surest ways to control the Negro is to control his education." (Roy Wilkins) Milwaukee's 22,000 Negro children are controlled in 30 inferior, segregated schools.

Don't talk it. DO IT! MARCH

Fight INFERIOR SCHOOLS in the Milwaukee March toward Freedom and Independence, Aug. 28, 2 p. m., 12 and Lloyd.

-- Milwaukee March Executive Committee, 2944 N. 9th Street --

Questions

Document 2. Flier recruiting residents for a march protesting segregated schools.

1. Working with a partner, explain the main message of the cartoon in your own words. (Hint: "core" refers to Milwaukee's Black neighborhood; "foundry" is a factory where people make things out of metal.)

2. List adjectives that describe the emotions the characters in the cartoon might be feeling. Which clues make you think that is what they are feeling?

3. What does the quotation from Roy Wilkins (to the right of the cartoon) mean? Who was in control in Milwaukee? Who didn't have control? What are some other words for control?

4. Aside from education, list three other things that will affect the life you'll live as an adult. Which one is the most important? Why? Explain your reasoning to your partner.

5. On another sheet of paper, draw a cartoon illustrating a social issue that you care about. What message are you trying to get across? How does your cartoon communicate that main message?

Milwaukee School Boycott, May 18, 1964.

Goals
Students analyze a political flier and a video clip, discover their main messages, and try to imagine what they would do in similar circumstances today.

Central Questions
Why did Milwaukee civil rights leaders call for a school boycott? What sacrifices are involved in direct actions like school boycotts?

Background Information:
Despite the 1954 *Brown v. Board of Education* decision declaring racial segregation illegal, a 1960 survey of Milwaukee schools found that schools in the central city were 90 percent Black. In March 1964, community activists, including attorney Lloyd Barbee, Milwaukee Common Council member Vel Phillips, and Father James Groppi organized the Milwaukee United School Integration Committee (MUSIC).

Parents were distressed by the vast differences in quality between majority Black and majority white schools. Another point of contention was "intact busing," or transporting African American students to all-white schools but keeping them in segregated classrooms, cafeterias, and activities. Many Black children were also tracked into vocational classes instead of business or college prep classes.

In 1964, MUSIC organized a one-day boycott of predominantly Black schools for May 18, the tenth anniversary of the U.S. Supreme Court's *Brown v. Board* decision. Instead of going to school, students attended Freedom Schools, where they learned about segregation, racism, and discrimination. The majority of Milwaukee's Black, inner-city school population (11,000 or roughly 60 percent) stayed out of school, and about 8,500 attended the Freedom Schools.

In October 1965, after seeing few significant changes, MUSIC organized a three-day boycott. By then, Barbee had filed a lawsuit charging the Milwaukee School Board with practicing discrimination, and the issue was tied up in the courts. Milwaukee's civil rights leaders shifted focus to fair housing and other equal opportunity issues.

Documents Used in This Lesson:
1. May 18, 1964 "Keep Your Children Out of School" flier.
   http://wihist.org/12iziaC
2. Five-minute news film clip on school boycotts and segregation, May 18, 1964. The first 1:50 seconds have no sound. At 1:50, Lloyd Barbee is interviewed for two minutes about the success of the boycott. The remaining two minutes of the video can be skipped.
   http://wihist.org/1yrlmXx

This lesson could be used in conjunction with Lesson 2, School Segregation in Milwaukee in the 1960s (p. 13), or Lesson 9, School Segregation in Missippi (p. 50).

Document 1: May 18, 1964 "Keep Your Children Out of School" flier.
http://wihist.org/12iziaC

KEEP YOUR CHILDREN OUT OF SCHOOL

Because

▷ Milwaukee schools are in fact segregated

▷ Negro children are receiving inferior education

▷ Almost one year of NAACP, CORE, and NNNPC efforts have met with continuous refusal to even recognize segregation in Milwaukee schools. The School Board in its current work sessions, has not yet begun to deal with the problem.

▷ The School Board continues to segregate 37 classes of Negro children who are bussed to 'white schools.'

A one day mass student withdrawal has been called by the Milwaukee United School Integration Committee (MUSIC) which includes all the civil rights groups and many church and fraternal groups. The withdrawal will protest and dramatize the evils of our segregated schools and the inferior education offered to our children.

Join thousands of Milwaukee parents who feel morally obligated to withdraw their children from school on Monday, May 18, 1964, in support of

FREEDOM DAY
MAY 18th

to commemorate the tenth anniversary of the U. S. Supreme Court's school desegregation decision.

Send your children to FREEDOM SCHOOLS which will be staffed by qualified persons who will offer them a full and enriching experience in the areas of freedom, democracy, and the achievements of Negroes in American civic, scientific, military, legal, educational, and cultural life.

A Freedom Day Hootenanny will also be held for the benefit of your children who attend the Freedom schools.

Stand with Milwaukee's civil rights' demand for integration of our schools and true equality of educational opportunities in the inner core.

Don't be intimidated! For further information call 374-6720. You will be assisted in every way. What will you do to HELP?

MILWAUKEE UNITED SCHOOL INTEGRATION COMMITTEE (MUSIC)

2944 North 9th Street   Milwaukee, Wisconsin   53206   Telephone 374-6720

Questions

Document 1: May 18, 1964 "Keep Your Children Out of School" flier.

Working in a small group, investigate the flier and answer the questions together. Reach agreement on a single answer to each question.

1. Who created the flier and who was its target audience? What evidence do you see on the flier to support your answers?

   Creator:

   Audience:

2. List in your own words the problems that organizers point out on the flier. Choose two problems you think are the most serious.

3. Think of two or three issues that people are protesting today. Choose one. If you were asked to boycott school in order to protest it, would you do it? Why or why not?

4. Can you imagine an issue that everybody in your group would skip school to protest? Describe it, and explain why it's more important than suffering the consequences of skipping school.

Document 2. News film clip on school boycotts and segregation, May 18, 1964.
http://wihist.org/12iziaC

Copyright Journal Broadcast Group. Provided by the Wisconsin Historical Society and Archives of the University of Wisconsin-Milwaukee Libraries

Questions

Document 2: News film clip on school boycotts and segregation, May 18, 1964.

Working with a partner, make notes on the following questions. Be prepared to share them with the class.

1. What's happening during the first two minutes when there's no sound? Make a list of the types of places shown and the activities you see happening there.

2. If the video had been used on the TV news, an announcer would have been talking over the first two minutes. What do you think would have been the announcer's main points? Consult your list from question 1.

3. Watch the brief interview with Lloyd Barbee. Why does he say the boycott is needed? Does he think it is succeeding? Do you think the man asking the questions supports the boycott, opposes it, or doesn't take sides? Why do you think that?

4. On another sheet, create your own script to go with the silent portion of the video. While the teacher shows the video read it aloud as if you were the newscaster.

Marching Across Milwaukee's 16th Street Bridge

Goals

Students begin to understand the fair housing marches of 1967-68, examine the motivations of participants, and investigate what fair housing means.

Central Questions

Why did civil rights leaders organize the marches and what happened? What is the Fair Housing law of 1968? What happens when civil rights and property rights conflict? What are some benefits and challenges of a diverse community?

Background Information

In 1967, Milwaukee neighborhoods had been segregated by law for decades. The Menominee River industrial district, just south of today's I-94, separated the African American neighborhood on the north from the exclusively white neighborhoods of South Milwaukee. The 16th Street Bridge (sometimes called the 16th Street Viaduct) connected the two.

On August 29, 1967, roughly 250 protesters led by Father James Groppi marched across the 16th Street Bridge toward a park on the south side to protest segregation and demand fair housing laws. While a similar march the night before had remained peaceful, the August 29 protest was greeted by 13,000 white residents carrying clubs, hurling glass bottles, and shouting racial slurs and profanities.

When police introduced tear gas, the 250 protesters returned north only to find their headquarters, the NAACP Freedom House, ablaze. Milwaukee Police claimed they heard shots fired inside and tear-gassed the building, which caught fire. No shooters or weapons were found, and today it is widely believed that police officers purposefully caused the fire.

Civil rights activists organized daily marches for 200 consecutive nights to demand a fair housing law. After the assassination of Martin Luther King Jr., in April 1968, the US Congress passed a national fair housing law. On April 30, 1968, the Milwaukee Common Council followed with its own ordinance.

After the Fair Housing Act passed, many white residents moved out of the city to the suburbs. Milwaukee remains one of the most segregated cities in the nation today. See the lesson plan, "Segregation in Milwaukee Today," (p. 43) for related content.

Documents Used in This Lesson:

1. Two-minute news film clip of the housing march, likely the night of August 29, 1967.
   http://wihist.org/1yuot15
   (This clip has no audio track; a newscaster would have been talking over it.)
2. Excerpt from the Fair Housing Act passed in 1968.
   http://www.justice.gov/crt/about/hce/title8.php

Document 1: Two-minute news film clip of the housing march, likely the night of August 29, 1967.
http://wihist.org/1yuot15

This short clip has no sound; a newscaster would have been talking over it.

Example of hate mail sent to Father Groppi that summer: http://wihist.org/1wL2JQx

GROPPI,
    YOU BETTER NOT TRY
TO COME DOWN TO THE
SOUTH SIDE OR WE'LL
MAKE THINGS <u>HOT</u> FOR
YOU IF YOU CROSS THAT
GULLY. WE DONT WANT
ANY NIGGERS DOWN
HERE. THE SOUTH SIDE
IS FOR <u>WHITES ONLY</u> +
WE INTEND TO KEEP
IT THAT WAY + THERE'S
NOTHING YOU CAN DO
ABOUT IT SO DONT EVEN
TRY.
    A SOUTH SIDER

Questions

Document 1: Two-minute news film clip of the housing march, likely the night of August 29, 1967.

On August 29, 1967, 250 protesters led by Father James Groppi marched across the 16th Street Bridge toward a park on the south side to protest segregation and demand fair housing laws. They were met by 13,000 white residents carrying clubs, hurling glass bottles, and shouting racial slurs and profanities. This video from that night has no sound track. Watch it with a partner and answer the following questions.

1. List the different types of people you see in the first thirty seconds. Where do you think they are? What is happening?

2. Look closely at the people shown between the 15- and 30-second marks. What do you think they are saying, based on their actions and facial features?

3. From what you can see in the video, did the police act properly or improperly? Why do you say that?

4. Imagine you are one of the marchers in the video. Write Tweets or text messages to your friends about what is happening to you. Write one from each scene in the video and assume they are happening a few minutes apart.

Document 2: excerpt from the Fair Housing law (Title VIII of the Civil Rights Act of 1968).
http://www.justice.gov/crt/about/hce/title8.php

Sec. 804. [42 U.S.C. 3604] Discrimination in sale or rental of housing and other prohibited practices

As made applicable by section 803 of this title and except as exempted by sections 803(b) and 807 of this title, it shall be unlawful--

(a) To refuse to sell or rent after the making of a bona fide offer, or to refuse to negotiate for the sale or rental of, or otherwise make unavailable or deny, a dwelling to any person because of race, color, religion, sex, familial status, or national origin.

(b) To discriminate against any person in the terms, conditions, or privileges of sale or rental of a dwelling, or in the provision of services or facilities in connection therewith, because of race, color, religion, sex, familial status, or national origin.

(c) To make, print, or publish, or cause to be made, printed, or published any notice, statement, or advertisement, with respect to the sale or rental of a dwelling that indicates any preference, limitation, or discrimination based on race, color, religion, sex, handicap, familial status, or national origin, or an intention to make any such preference, limitation, or discrimination.

(d) To represent to any person because of race, color, religion, sex, handicap, familial status, or national origin that any dwelling is not available for inspection, sale, or rental when such dwelling is in fact so available.

(e) For profit, to induce or attempt to induce any person to sell or rent any dwelling by representations regarding the entry or prospective entry into the neighborhood of a person or persons of a particular race, color, religion, sex, handicap, familial status, or national origin.

Questions

Document 2: excerpt from the Fair Housing law (Title VIII of the Civil Rights Act of 1968).

With a partner, investigate these questions, come up with an answer that you both agree upon, and be ready to discuss them with the class.

1. What's the most important phrase in the opening four lines?

2. Choose two of the sections (a through e) and rewrite them in simpler, shorter ways that somebody younger than you could understand.

3. Should people be able to live wherever they want if they can afford it? Why? Should landlords be able to reject anybody they want, for any reason they want? Why? Do these two ideas conflict? How could you resolve any conflict that you see?

4. Think about your school, your neighborhood, and your community. Do you see people from many different racial and ethnic backgrounds? List three good things about living in a racially diverse community. List three hard things about living in a diverse community.

How Young People Made a Difference in Milwaukee

Goals

Students learn about teenagers' participation in Milwaukee's civil rights struggle by examining a NAACP Youth Council press release and listening to an interview with a woman who marched during the years 1963–68, when she was a high school student.

Central Questions

How and why did the NAACP Youth Council protest? Why did individuals decide to join and take action? What role did the Commandos have within the group and why were they necessary? What role did Father Groppi play?

Background Information

Created in 1936, Milwaukee's NAACP Youth Council played a large part in the city's desegregation efforts. In the early 1960s, as lunch counter sit-ins erupted across the South, the Youth Council adopted a strategy of local direct action. In 1963 the council campaigned against job discrimination at Marc's Big Boy restaurants, protested against the all-white Eagles Club, and demonstrated in support of a fair housing law. Father James Groppi became an advisor to the group in 1965.

The Youth Council established its headquarters at 2026 North Fifth Street in 1966. As tensions rose in Milwaukee, the group formed a security unit known as Youth Council Commandos to protect marchers from violence. Eventually, many Commandos parted ways with the Youth Council to create a separate organization that became one of the city's most effective social service agencies from the late 1960s until the early 1980s.

Documents Used in this Lesson:

1. NAACP Youth Council flier, "Why We Demonstrate," describing the 1963 protest against Big Boy restaurant. http://wihist.org/18VbblZ
2. 2007 Interview with Mary Arms about being part of the NAACP Youth Council, 1963-1968. http://wihist.org/1NbSJmm

The most useful clips to play in class are:

17:40–19:50. She describes facing the Ku Klux Klan in Milwaukee in 1963, being injured by a cherry bomb, being tear-gassed, and describes other demonstrations with the NAACP Youth Council.

20:40–25:15. She describes starting fair housing work with Father Groppi, how Groppi and the Commandos planned march routes and assessed risks, and the power of freedom songs.

25:15–26:50. She recalls the death and funeral of Martin Luther King Jr.

26:50–30:55. She remembers how she coined the name "Commandos," explains why the council formed the group, discusses Father Groppi, recalls the roles of girls in the Commando-ettes, and recounts police infiltration.

On the interview web page, you can either play the audio MP3 or display a typed transcript.

Document 1, 1963 NAACP Youth Council flier, "Why We Demonstrate."
http://wihist.org/18VbblZ

WHY WE DEMONSTRATE

On March 5, 1963, a member of the Milwaukee NAACP Youth Council applied for
a job at Marc's Big Boy's store located at 2207 East North Avenue.
He was told he would be called the next day and informed whether he was hired.
Not hearing from Marc's Big Boy, the youth called, on March 7th, 1963, to
ascertain whether he was employed. A manager at Marc's Big Boy informed our
member the job was filled.

The manager stated Marc's Big Boy policy prohibited hiring Negroes at the
2207 East North Avenue store. He further stated that a neat Negro bus boy who
was a good worker had been working at the 2207 East North Avenue store but was
fired because business fell off due to his employment.

The NAACP Youth Council's special employment sub-committee conferred with
Marc's Big Boy's Supervisor of Personnel on March 11, 1963. He stated Marc's
Big Boy employed a few Negro bus boys, 2 cooks, and a few general food prepar-
ers. No Negro managers, shift managers, or hostesses are employed by Marc's
Big Boy. However, one waitress is employed at the downtown store where she is
acceptable.

Since the Supervisor of Personnel made no effort to redress this wrong or
further communicate with us, we contacted Mr. Ben Marcus, the owner of Marc's
Big Boy, by letter on March 13, 1963. In this letter we emphasized our position that Marc's Big Boy employment pattern is not integrated. We also informed Mr. Marcus that qualified Negro young people are ready to fulfill available
managerial jobs as well as hostess and waitress positions. Mr. Marcus never
acknowledged our communication.

We PROTEST Marc's Big Boy's discriminatory practices by not employing Negroes
in all job classifications.

We PROTEST Marc's Big Boy's discriminatory practices by not employing Negroes
at all stores.

We MAINTAIN that Marc's Big Boy is not complying with the law by hiring all
applicants for all jobs in all locations, without regard to race, creed or
color.

We URGE the public to aid us in securing equal employment opportunities
for all workers in the City of Milwaukee.

We IMPLORE citizens of Milwaukee to call upon employers to cease token
employment of Negroes in stereotype positions, "safe" locations, as well as
practicing blantant discrimination.

Milwaukee NAACP Youth Council
815 West North Avenue
Milwaukee 5, Wisconsin

Questions

Document 1: NAACP Youth Council flier, "Why We Demonstrate," describing the 1963 protest against Big Boy restaurant.

With a partner, read the flier and agree on a single answer to each of the first three questions.

1. What's the main message of the flier? What is it trying to do?

2. Who created it? Who is the intended audience?

3. Turn each of its last five paragraphs into a short phrase that somebody younger than you could understand. Start each one with, "Marc's Big Boy should…"

4. Take sides in a debate about the issue of race and hiring. One of you is a job applicant who has been turned down because of your race—and you think that's unfair. The other is a store manager who believes that white customers don't want to be waited on by Black waitresses or waiters and needs to keep the customers happy.

Document 2: 2007 Interview with Mary Arms about being part of the NAACP Youth Council, 1963-1968. http://wihist.org/1NbSJmm

Excerpts from transcript of oral history interview with Mary Arms

1. "Oh that was scary. The Eagles Club, that's my first time ever seeing the Ku Klux Klan, despite all I went through in Mississippi, was the first time I saw the Klan was, they were marching against us across the street on Wisconsin Avenue when we were marching for the Eagle's Club. And then going out to Wauwatosa … we got cherry bombed and both of us just dazed, knocked us down, because when I woke up, it's like, I always said when I woke up, I still had Junior's hand. He was laying beside me. And we got up and took off running … it was when we were protesting out in Wauwatosa in front of Judge Cannon's house. And, you know, naturally we had all the hecklers out there, throw things at you, and they threw that cherry bomb and some kind of bomb, it just exploded. Or a firecracker, it was so loud it just knocked us flat. That was my first so-called injury. My mother used to, when we would be tear gassed, we'd come home hours afterwards and bring tears to their eyes. You know they could smell it when we come …"

2. "We needed somebody to protect us from the police. The police would not protect us. They would let people come in the line and do things, you know so we needed protection … the name Commandos, I don't know. I can't even remember how I come up with the name Commandos, but it was me. As a matter of fact Shirley had to remind me, "Mary you're the one, you remember?" and I would say "yeah, but I, I don't know what I was thinking about." They looked like it when they used to wear those tams and the combat boots, and the camouflage. That's how they originally dressed. I said they looked like Commandos, you know, like the Marines or somebody, you know the Green Berets and all of those people. So I called them Commandos and it stuck …"

3. "That was basically our job [the Commando-ettes], and watch out for, you know, different things we need to call to the Commandos attention. And we didn't want people in the line with weapons or people that come to be violent. We heard of the police actually putting somebody in, just to cause a disruption so they can come in and beat us up. We had to watch out for things like that. That's basically for the Commando-ettes. … We fought just as hard. We were right there by their side."

Questions

Document 2: 2007 Interview with Mary Arms about being part of the NAACP Youth Council, 1963-1968.

Listen to the last thirteen minutes of the interview, beginning at 17:40, and then answer the first three questions with a partner. Complete questions 4 and 5 on your own. Question 6 might be homework.

1. When was the interview conducted? When did the events that Arms describes happen? Roughly how many years had passed between the two? Does that affect what you hear?

2. How did Arms participate in Milwaukee's Civil Rights Movement when she was a teenager? List five specific activities she remembers from when she was your age.

3. Why did the Youth Council form the Commandos? What was the purpose?

4. Compare the interview format with other kinds of historical documents you've seen, like a letter, a newspaper article, or an autobiography. How does listening to an interview affect you differently than reading something?

5. Imagine you are a Youth Council member and write a fictional diary entry based on any one of the episodes that Arms recalled. Make up any details you need to.

6. Interview a parent or a grandparent. If they were in Milwaukee (or another big city) during the 1960s, ask them what they did during the marches and protests, how they knew about them, and what they remember. If they were someplace else, ask them about things they did when they were your age.

Vel Phillips and the Struggle for Fair Housing

Goals

Students watch a four-minute video of the Milwaukee Common Council postponing action on Alderwoman Vel Phillips's proposed fair housing ordinance, analyze key provisions of the Fair Housing Act of 1968, and debate the conflict between property rights and civil rights.

Central Questions

What necessitated the passage of the Fair Housing Act of 1968? Why were some people opposed to the act? What happened to African Americans in inner cities after this law was passed? Did passing the act end segregation?

Background Information

Until the 1960s, discriminatory laws forced nearly all African Americans in Milwaukee to live in a single neighborhood just north and northwest of downtown. Ninety percent of Milwaukee subdivisions had been planned out with regulations prohibiting the sale of property to people of color; and informal agreements among realtors, lenders, and landlords reinforced those restrictions. This was not illegal until 1968; many, if not most, US cities were similarly segregated.

Black residents who tried to move out of the central city were met by landlords who refused to rent to them or banks that wouldn't give mortgages. When they tried to rent vacant apartments, the landlords told them that the spaces had suddenly been rented to others, or that prices and rents were much higher than had been publicly advertised.

In 1962, Alderwoman Vel Phillips introduced to the Milwaukee Common Council the first ordinance intended to reverse this sort of discrimination. The council voted to defeat it 18-1, her vote being the only one in favor. The same vote reoccurred three more times over the next six years. Finally, in 1967-68, Milwaukee's NAACP Youth Council picketed the homes of alders and marched for 200 consecutive nights to demand a fair housing law. In April 1968, after the assassination of Martin Luther King Jr., the US Congress passed a national fair housing law. On April 30, 1968, the Milwaukee Common Council followed with its own ordinance.

As neighborhoods opened up to African Americans, thousands of white residents left the city: in 1960, Milwaukee had 668,000 white residents, but in 2000, it had only 298,000. Although segregation has been illegal in housing, schools, employment, and other areas of US life for nearly half a century, Milwaukee remains one of the most segregated cities in the nation today.

Documents Used in This Lesson:

1. News film clip of a Milwaukee Common Council meeting where Alderwoman Vel Phillips urges action on a fair housing ordinance, September 19, 1967.
    http://wihist.org/1yqyrmB
2. Excerpt from the Fair Housing law, Title VIII of the Civil Rights Act of 1968.
    http://wihist.org/1xO1hLW

Document 1: News film clip of a Milwaukee Common Council meeting, September 19, 1967.
http://wihist.org/1yqyrmB

This four-minute video clip shows what Milwaukee Common Council meetings were like at the height of the fair housing effort in 1967. Because the film is unedited raw footage, it skips around a little.

In the first minute, Alderwoman Vel Phillips requests that the Milwaukee Common Council take action on her proposed ordinance to guarantee fair housing to the city's residents. Father James Groppi and a number of NAACP Youth Council Commandos rise to applaud when she finishes.

At 1:25, Alderman Robert Dwyer responds by proposing that her ordinance be left to a committee. He objects to what he terms her "veiled threat" and questions the motives of the demonstrators.

At 3:25, Phillips summarizes the national importance of the Milwaukee fair housing struggle and urges that the ordinance not be held up in the city attorney's office "until things simmer down, because things are not going to simmer down."

Questions

Document 1: News film clip of a Milwaukee Common Council meeting, September 19, 1967.

1. The opening speaker is Alderwoman Vel Phillips. What is her main point? How would you describe her demeanor and behavior toward the other council members she's addressing?

2. At 1:25, Alderman Robert Dwyer replies to Phillips. What are his main points? How would you describe his demeanor and behavior toward Phillips?

3. Phillips was the only woman and the only African American on the Common Council. Imagine that you are in her position. Smartphones didn't exist back then, but imagine they did and compose three Tweets or text messages during the meeting about what is happening. The audience who will read them includes the Commandos who stand and clap and other supporters.

4. What surprised you in this video? What did you realize or learn for the first time when watching it?

Document 2: excerpt from the Fair Housing law (Title VIII of the Civil Rights Act of 1968). http://wihist.org/1xO1hLW

In April 1968, six months after the events depicted in the video, the US government passed a law prohibiting discrimination in housing. The Milwaukee Common Council followed suit.

Sec. 804. [42 U.S.C. 3604] Discrimination in sale or rental of housing and other prohibited practices

As made applicable by section 803 of this title and except as exempted by sections 803(b) and 807 of this title, it shall be unlawful--

(a) To refuse to sell or rent after the making of a bona fide offer, or to refuse to negotiate for the sale or rental of, or otherwise make unavailable or deny, a dwelling to any person because of race, color, religion, sex, familial status, or national origin.

(b) To discriminate against any person in the terms, conditions, or privileges of sale or rental of a dwelling, or in the provision of services or facilities in connection therewith, because of race, color, religion, sex, familial status, or national origin.

(c) To make, print, or publish, or cause to be made, printed, or published any notice, statement, or advertisement, with respect to the sale or rental of a dwelling that indicates any preference, limitation, or discrimination based on race, color, religion, sex, handicap, familial status, or national origin, or an intention to make any such preference, limitation, or discrimination.

(d) To represent to any person because of race, color, religion, sex, handicap, familial status, or national origin that any dwelling is not available for inspection, sale, or rental when such dwelling is in fact so available.

(e) For profit, to induce or attempt to induce any person to sell or rent any dwelling by representations regarding the entry or prospective entry into the neighborhood of a person or persons of a particular race, color, religion, sex, handicap, familial status, or national origin.

Questions

Document 2: excerpt from the Fair Housing law (Title VIII of the Civil Rights Act of 1968).

With a partner, investigate these questions, come up with an answer that you both agree upon, and be ready to discuss them with the class.

1. What's the most important phrase in the opening four lines?

2. Choose two of the sections (a through e) and rewrite them in simpler, shorter ways that somebody younger than you could understand.

3. Debate with your partner: Should people be able to live wherever they want, if they can afford it? Why? Should landlords be able to reject anybody they want, for any reason they want? Why? Do these two ideas conflict? How could you resolve any conflict that you see?

4. Think about your school, your neighborhood, and your community. Do you see people from lots of different racial and ethnic backgrounds? List three good things about living in a racially diverse community. List three hard things about living in a diverse community.

Busing in Milwaukee Public Schools since 1979

Goals

Students examine arguments for and against busing by watching a ten-minute video, comparing Milwaukee's experience with that of Charlotte-Mecklenburg, N.C., and analyzing two 1983 letters to the editor.

Central Questions

What are the arguments for and against busing as a way to integrate schools? Why do people oppose it? What benefits come from it? Did it actually end segregation in Milwaukee schools?

Background Information

Despite the 1954 *Brown v. Board of Education* decision, which declared segregated schools illegal, a 1960 survey in Milwaukee found that schools in the central city were 90 percent Black. In March 1964, community activists, including attorney Lloyd Barbee, Milwaukee Common Council member Vel Phillips, and Father James Groppi organized the Milwaukee United School Integration Committee (MUSIC). In May 1964, MUSIC organized a boycott of predominantly Black schools, which garnered participation by more than half of the city's African American students. MUSIC also challenged segregated schools through picketing, demonstrations, and other direct actions.

In 1965, when the school board still refused to comply with *Brown v. Board of Education*, Barbee filed a lawsuit charging the board with practicing discrimination. The city fought the lawsuit for 14 years. In 1976, US district court judge John Reynolds ruled that the city had "acted to create and maintain unlawful racial segregation in the Milwaukee public school system" and in 1979, the US Supreme Court confirmed his decision. Milwaukee was forced to desegregate its schools.

The desegregation plan involved redistricting, creating specialty ("magnet") schools, and busing. The majority of students who chose integrated, specialty schools were white, while 80 percent of those being bused out of their neighborhoods were Black. In 1987, after hundreds of thousands of white residents had fled Milwaukee, the court ruled that suburban districts had to participate. For another decade, several thousand urban Black students were bused to suburban schools each year. In the late 1990s, busing was largely abandoned in favor of charter schools and other "school choice" programs, like vouchers, which use tax dollars for private school tuition. Today, the Milwaukee public schools are again largely segregated.

Documents Used in This Lesson:

1. Ten-minute video "The Battle for Busing," *New York Times*. Sept. 9, 2013. A fine overview that focuses on Charlotte, N.C., the first city to implement busing for integration. There is no transcript, so students should take a few notes while watching it.
   http://wihist.org/1vFsM9V
2. Anti-busing letters to the editor, *Milwaukee Journal*, December 29, 1983.
   http://wihist.org/1w0xpNL

Document 1: "Battle for Busing" *New York Times.* Sept. 9, 2013, video, 10:18.
http://wihist.org/1vFsM9V

No transcript is provided. Here's an outline, to help students take notes

0:00-0:55   history of segregated schools and busing as a solution

1:05-4:00   1971, busing starts in Charlotte, N.C.

4:00-5:30   successes of initial busing program

5:40-6:15   the results researchers saw a few years later

6:20-7:45   1990s opponents of busing

8:10-9:30   effects of ending busing

9:45-10:05   two systems of education in the United States today

Questions

Document 1: "Battle for Busing" *New York Times*, Sept. 9, 2013.

Because no transcript is provided for this short video, take notes on a separate piece of paper. Then find a partner and agree on answers to these questions, which we'll discuss afterward.

1. At 1:21, Arthur Griffin starts talking about the segregated schools he attended, before busing. Name three examples he gives of how all-Black schools were worse off than all-white ones. Why were the city's schools segregated?

2. At 5:40, Dr. Rosaline Mickelson explains some things that happened when students began attending integrated schools. List three of them. Why would those things happen in an integrated school but not in a segregated one?

3. Identify the part of the video that impressed or affected you the most. Why?

4. Today, Milwaukee-area schools are segregated in the same way the video describes at 9:45. How do you think that happened? What do you think should be done about it?

Document 2: Anti-busing letters to the editor, *Milwaukee Journal*, December 29, 1983.
http://wihist.org/1w0xpNL

Just what kind of dictators do the Milwaukee School Board members think they are? Who are they to say that we in the rural communities must bus some of our children to Milwaukee schools?

Perhaps they don't realize that they are trying to do more than exchange students from one side of Milwaukee to another. They are trying to uproot students who have attended schools in a rural atmosphere and ship them to a completely different environment.

I personally feel that no way, come hell or high water, will my child ever be bused to Milwaukee to attend school. And I believe that as the integration issue progresses, the Milwaukee School Board will find many more parents such as myself, long-time residents of the "country," who will oppose such a proposal.

If Milwaukee wishes to bus some of its children to outlying area schools and Milwaukee parents are willing to accept that, then I am sure those students will be welcome in our school systems. But don't try to force us to send our children to Milwaukee. I, for one, will never permit it.

DARRYL GUST
Pewaukee

I don't want to go to school in Milwaukee! I like it where I am. The metro busing plan is unfair. They're *not* going to force me to go to school so far away from home. I'm *not* getting up one hour earlier to ride a bus to school in an unfamiliar area; it's unfair! Also, how much is this going to cost my parents? Are people aware of the money it takes to run buses 10-15 miles to and from schools every day?

Most school districts are concerned about their budgets. They "cut" good teachers every year because of a lack of funds. Proposing to spend thousands of dollars per day to benefit mainly Milwaukee's students lacks common sense, in my opinion.

The metro busing plan is an unnecessary waste of taxpayers' money and disregards students' needs and rights, both in the city and suburbs.

Perhaps school board members should get up one hour earlier to ride the bus to their jobs each day!

Greendale   **JULIE KRESKE**

Questions

Document 2: Anti-busing letters to the editor, *Milwaukee Journal*, December 29, 1983.

Working with a partner or in a small group, agree on answers to the following questions.

1. List two reasons that Darryl Gust gives in Letter 1 for his opposition to busing students from the suburbs into the city. Now list reasons given in Letter 2. Are those reasons more important, in your opinion, than the benefits that Mickelson listed at 5:40 in the video?

2. Should a higher level of government, like the state or a county, ever be able to overrule a lower one, like a town or a village? On what sorts of issues? Should any government be able to take away an individual's freedom? When?

3. Fold a blank sheet into thirds and head the columns, "Surprise, Realize, and Visualize." In the left column, describe something about the two letters that surprised you. In the center, explain something you realized after discussing the first two questions with your partner. In the right-hand column, imagine a school where people of different races and backgrounds were treated equally and fairly. How would people be different?

Segregation in Milwaukee Today

Goals

Students discover the effects of de facto segregation by examining maps that show race and income distribution. Using the Anti-Defamation League's "Pyramid of Hate", they identify prejudice in their own lives and imagine steps they can take to change it. Although this lesson is focused on Milwaukee, its sources work for any location in the United States.

Central Questions

How does life in Milwaukee today compare with life in segregated Mississippi in 1964? What is de facto segregation? What can we do about it?

Background Information

Fifty years ago, Mississippi was considered the most segregated place in the country. Today, Milwaukee is called the most segregated place in the country. But conditions in the two places are radically different.

In Mississippi in 1964, government-sponsored (de jure) segregation was enforced through laws, economics, and public opinion. The races were separated, African-Americans had dramatically lower standards of living, and challenges to the status quo were met with violence.

Something quite different happens in Milwaukee today. Our laws legally prohibit racial segregation in housing, jobs, and schools. Yet most residents of the Milwaukee area live in very segregated communities, and Black neighborhoods have much higher poverty rates than white ones. This is called de facto segregation, meaning that it's still a fact, even though laws do not cause it. De facto segregation is created and maintained by ideas about other races inside people's minds, rather than by forces such as laws, police, or terrorist groups.

Documents Used in This Lesson:

1. Demographics Research Group, Racial Dot Map for Milwaukee area, 2013 (click to zoom in).
    http://wihist.org/1HW1AZK
2. *New York Times* "Mapping Poverty in America," map of Milwaukee neighborhoods by poverty rate, 2014.
    (click to zoom in)
    http://wihist.org/1rSAi1O
3. Anti-Defamation League's "Pyramid of Hate."
    http://wihist.org/1wlv2Vt

Document 1: Demographics Research Group, Racial Dot Map for Milwaukee area, 2013.
http://wihist.org/1HW1AZK

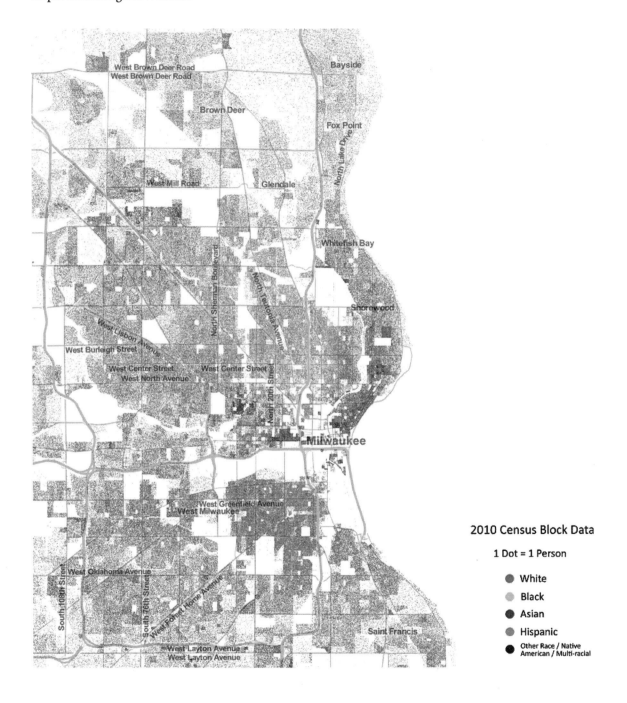

Note: the online version of the map is color- coded.

Document 2: *New York Times* "Mapping Poverty in America," map of Milwaukee neighborhoods by poverty rate, 2014.
http://wihist.org/1rSAi1O

Questions

Documents 1 and 2: maps showing segregation in Milwaukee today.

With a partner or in a small group, brainstorm answers to these questions:

1. Examine Document 1, the racial groups map. Where is downtown? Where is your school? Where do most Black people live? Where do most Hispanic people live? Where do most white people live? Are the races segregated in Milwaukee?

2. If the Civil Rights Act made segregation illegal 50 years ago, how can this be? List three things that encourage segregated neighborhoods.

3. Examine Document 2, the poverty rates map. Which neighborhoods have the most poverty? Which ones have the least? How does income correspond to housing segregation in the Milwaukee area?

4. Until 1950, nearly all Milwaukee's factories and jobs were located close to downtown, along railroad corridors and next to today's I-94 highway. After the 1960s, many employers closed those century-old factories and relocated them to the suburbs. What color are suburbs on the poverty rates map? Why don't inner-city residents commute out to jobs in places like Brookfield, Oak Creek, or Brown Deer?

Document 3: Anti-Defamation League's "Pyramid of Hate."

Pyramid of Hate

GENOCIDE
The act or intent to deliberately and systematically annihilate an entire people

BIAS-MOTIVATED VIOLENCE

INDIVIDUAL
Murder
Rape
Assault
Threats

COMMUNITY
Arson
Terrorism
Vandalism
Desecration

DISCRIMINATION

Economic Discrimination
Employment Discrimination
Educational Discrimination

Political Discrimination
Housing Discrimination
Segregation

INDIVIDUAL ACTS OF PREJUDICE

Bullying
Ridicule

Name-calling
Social Avoidance

Slurs/Epithets
De-humanization

BIAS
Stereotyping • Insensitive remarks • Belittling jokes • Non-inclusive language
Justifying biases by seeking out like-minded people
Accepting negative information/screening out positive information

Document 3: Anti-Defamation League's "Pyramid of Hate."

Read the following story:

In one school, a group of four boys began whispering and laughing about another boy in their school who they thought was gay. They began making comments when they walked by him in the hall.

Soon they started insulting him with anti-gay slurs. By the end of the month, they had taken their harassment to another level, tripping him when he walked by and pushing him into a locker while they yelled slurs.

Sometime during the next month, they increased the seriousness of their conduct — they surrounded him and two boys held his arms while the others hit and kicked him. Eventually, one of the boys threatened to bring his father's gun into school the next day to kill the boy. At this point, another student overheard the threat and the police were notified.

Answer these questions on your own:

1. Could something like this happen at your school? What could have been done to stop the situation from escalating? Who should have stopped it? When?

2. Look at the "Pyramid of Hate" with a partner. Where does each act in the story of the gay student belong on the pyramid?

3. Have you ever encountered or witnessed acts of prejudice? What were they? Where do they belong on the pyramid?

4. How does the "Pyramid of Hate" connect to the segregation and poverty that the maps of Milwaukee show?

5. Write on a 3 x 5 card one way that you might change your own behavior when you witness prejudice. (The teacher will collect the cards and post them somewhere in the classroom as reminders for the next few days. Some classrooms have done this by having students assemble the cards into a "promise tree" or a mobile. Invite students to examine the ideas that the class wrote.)

PART TWO

Lessons about the Civil Rights Movement in the South

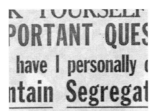

'I didn't know colored people could vote.'

Segregation in Mississippi in 1960

Goals

Students extract information from a map, a statistical table, and a photograph; synthesize their findings; and reach conclusions about the effects of state-sponsored segregation. This lesson could be paired with the lesson "Segregation in Milwaukee Today"(p. 43) to help students learn the difference between de jure and de facto segregation.

Central Questions

What was Jim Crow segregation like? How were Black people's lives different from white people's? What do maps, statistics, and images tell us about the past?

Background Information

Although slavery had ended 100 years earlier, African Americans in Mississippi had been kept in subjugation for decades through a system known as "Jim Crow."

In 1964, state and local laws separated whites and Blacks in housing, jobs, schools, churches, playgrounds, and all other aspects of social life. These discriminatory policies meant that African Americans had the worst jobs, lowest pay, poorest schools, and harshest living conditions. Most Black Mississippians had less than a sixth-grade education and worked at menial jobs, such as field hands or maids. More than 90 percent of African Americans were barred from voting in local, state or national elections, even in places where African Americans constituted a majority of the residents.

White supremacist politicians, police, and business leaders worked together to keep African Americans "in their place." Black Mississippians who challenged the system were arrested and jailed, punished by white employers, or attacked by terrorist groups like the Ku Klux Klan. Some were even killed for trying to vote or improve their lives.

Some people called this institutionalized racism "the Southern way of life." The law, the police, the courts, the church, the media, and the schools taught that Black people were dangerous and inferior to white people. Government officials at all levels deliberately passed laws to keep the races apart and keep control over African American people. This type of segregation is called de jure segregation, or segregation "by law."

Documents Used in This Lesson:

1. Map of Mississippi population distribution by race in 1960.
   http://wihist.org/1rWxISS
2. Tables of Mississippi occupations and income by race in 1960.
   http://wihist.org/1wn5ffw
3. Photograph of an African American neighborhood in Natchez, Mississippi, 1965.
   http://wihist.org/1AdxATU

Document 1: Map of Mississippi population distribution by race in 1960.
http://wihist.org/1rWxISS

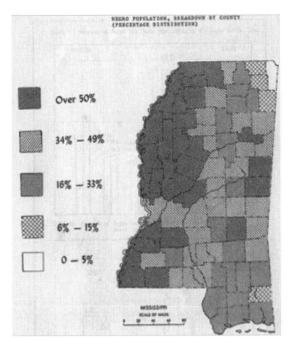

Document 2: Mississippi occupations and income by race in 1960. http://wihist.org/1wn5ffw

TABLE 14: INDUSTRY GROUPING OF EMPLOYED PERSONS, 1960 (PERCENTAGE) 17

INDUSTRY	NONWHITE				WHITE			
	State	Urban	Rural Non-farm	Rural Farm	State	Urban	Rural Non-farm	Rural Farm
Agriculture	34.9	3.1	36.0	76.5	12.8	1.2	8.4	47.1
Manufacturing	4.6	6.7	4.4	2.0	23.3	20.1	29.1	20.2
Wholesale trade	1.3	2.4	1.1	0.2	3.2	4.6	2.5	1.1
Mining	0.1	0.2	0.1	0.1	1.3	1.3	0.9	0.8
Transportation, Communications and other public utilities	4.0	3.6	3.3	1.5	4.8	6.1	3.3	2.8
Retail Trade	8.5	14.4	7.4	1.7	16.9	20.9	16.9	7.5
Service Industries	35.9	55.1	31.7	12.4	26.1	31.1	23.0	10.8
Industry not reported	2.1	2.6	1.9	1.5	1.9	2.2	1.7	1.8

Source: U.S. Bureau of the Census

TABLE 16: MEDIAN INCOME FOR PERSONS, 1950 AND 1960

RACE	1950			1960		
	State	Urban	Rural	State	Urban	Rural
White	$1,236	$1,826	$973	$2,023	$2,622	$1,065
Nonwhite	$ 440	$ 693	$390	$ 606	$ 871	$ 474

Source: U.S. Bureau of the Census

Questions

Documents 1 and 2: Map of population and tables of occupation and income by race, 1960.

With a partner, answer these questions. Discuss them afterward.

1. Examine the map of Mississippi. Where did most Black Mississippians live?

2. The western counties of the state, next to the Mississippi River, contained enormous cotton plantations owned mostly by white people but employing mostly Black tenant farmers. That region is called the Mississippi Delta. What kinds of jobs do you think were most common there?

3. Look at the first table. What types of jobs did most Black residents have? How about white residents?

4. Look at the second table. How much money did Black people make compared to white people? Express it as a percentage or a fraction.

5. Based on what you can learn from the map and tables, write five words that describe what life was like for Black Mississippians.

Document 3: Photo of African American neighborhood in Natchez, Mississippi, 1965.
http://wihist.org/1AdxATU

A caption on the back reads, "The city has no housing code and continues to ignore the slums of Natchez. No pavement, no streetlights, 10 outside flush toilets in 2 centrally located shanties shared by 114 people. The 125 persons living in this area share eight water faucets; of these 8, two are inside (installed by tenants) and 6 are outside."

Document 3: Photo of African American neighborhood in Natchez, Mississippi, 1965.

1. What are the three most important things you see in the picture?

2. What do you think the kids are talking about? Make up a conversation that they're having.

3. How do the picture, the caption, the map, and the tables connect with each other?

4. What does the photograph tell you that the map and the tables can't?

Segregated Schools: Winners and Losers

Goals

Students compare school segregation in Milwaukee and Mississippi during the 1960s, consider the relationship between knowledge and power, and reflect upon the value of education in their own lives.

Central Questions

How were segregated schools in Mississippi and Milwaukee similar? What's the relationship between a poor education and the choices people have in later life? How important is education in helping people shape their own lives?

Background Information

In 1896, the Supreme Court ruled in *Plessy v. Ferguson* that "separate but equal" facilities for Blacks and whites were legal as long as they were of the same quality. State and local officials quickly passed laws to separate the races in nearly all aspects of social life. Throughout the South, in particular, control of government, laws, courts, police, jobs, banks, business, media, and schools was quickly concentrated in the hands of a white elite.

By 1960, six decades of these laws and customs had left the majority of Black Mississippians uneducated and powerless. Most lived in rural areas, worked as field hands or domestic servants, and spent six years or less in school. Tens of thousands could not read or write. On average, Black workers earned about a third of what white workers earned. The white power structure relied on a huge labor force of intimidated, compliant workers; schools that taught white supremacy and kept African Americans down were key to the success of the unjust system. "I didn't know colored people could vote," a Black Mississippian told one Freedom Summer volunteer in 1964.

Meanwhile, in Milwaukee, most schools were more than 90 percent white, while those in the central city were 90 percent Black. Predominantly Black schools generally had poorer facilities, larger classes, and other problems similar to those in Mississippi.

In 1965, Milwaukee attorney Lloyd Barbee filed a lawsuit that challenged segregation in the city's public schools, the first of its kind in the nation. The suit claimed that the school board intentionally practiced discrimination in the public schools by drawing district boundaries based on segregated housing patterns and other discriminatory policies. For 14 years the city fought the suit, all the way to the US Supreme Court, but in March 1979 the case was settled and the school board agreed to implement a five-year desegregation plan. See Lessons 2 and 7 for more on Milwaukee's civil rights history.

Documents Used in this Lesson:

1. "What Is a Ruleville Education?" (1964).
   http://wihist.org/1DUD9vX
2. Mississippi occupations and income by race in 1960.
   http://wihist.org/1wn5ffw
3. Comments on Milwaukee schools by Black residents, 1965 (excerpts).
   http://wihist.org/1uUxFM6

Document 1: "What Is a Ruleville Education?" (Three paragraphs written by a visitor to the segregated high school in Ruleville, Miss., in 1964).

http://wihist.org/1DUD9vX

high school. I will list these problems
1) In the high school it is not uncommon to find classes with over sixty kids
in them. There are two with over seventy six. Another has ninety eight taught by
two teachers. There are four classes using the gym at the same time. This means
that there is little opportunity for discussion between teacher and student.
Quite often students have to sit two in one seat. In this kind of heat this kind
of classroom arrangement would make it impossible to learn anything. Along with
the overcrowded classrooms go the overcrowded school buses. This might not seem so
important, but in a rural school that takes people in from the plantations and
from places as far away as the outskirts of Shaw it is pretty important how the
students are transported.

of Ruleville had never seen a library or knew how to use one.
+ 3) (Principal has admitted to me in "confidence" that teachers are poorly
prepared to teach.) Generally they all go through a segregated Mississippi high
school and then get a two year certificate from a segregated Miss. college. With
this education they walk into classrooms with sixty people in them.
4) A couple of other problems that arise out of a lack of funds are poor
quality text books and no cooling facilities although students are in session
from July 5 to August 28. Teachers salaries are among the lowest in the United
States so there is not much attraction in going into the field. From the lot of
teachers that have been talked to, there seems to be little interest in teaching.
One of the students told that the Miss. history teacher spent most of the time
talking about the state flower and famous areas in the state.

Document 2: Mississippi occupations and income by race in 1960.

http://wihist.org/1wn5ffw

TABLE 16:   MEDIAN INCOME FOR PERSONS, 1950 AND 1960

RACE	1950			1960		
	State	Urban	Rural	State	Urban	Rural
White	$1,236	$1,826	$973	$2,023	$2,622	$1,065
Nonwhite	$ 440	$ 693	$390	$ 606	$ 871	$ 474

Source: U.S. Bureau of the Census

TABLE 14:   INDUSTRY GROUPING OF EMPLOYED PERSONS, 1960 (PERCENTAGE) 17

INDUSTRY	NONWHITE				WHITE			
	State	Urban	Rural Non-farm	Rural Farm	State	Urban	Rural Non-farm	Rural Farm
Agriculture	34.9	3.1	36.0	76.5	12.8	1.2	8.4	47.1
Manufacturing	4.6	6.7	4.4	2.0	23.3	20.1	29.1	20.2
Wholesale trade	1.3	2.4	1.1	0.2	3.2	4.6	2.5	1.1
Mining	0.1	0.2	0.1	0.1	1.3	1.3	0.9	0.8
Transportation, Communications and other public utilities	4.0	3.6	3.3	1.5	4.8	6.1	3.3	2.8
Retail Trade	8.5	14.4	7.4	1.7	16.9	20.9	16.9	7.5
Service Industries	35.9	55.1	31.7	12.4	26.1	31.1	23.0	10.8
Industry not reported	2.1	2.6	1.9	1.5	1.9	2.2	1.7	1.8

Source: U.S. Bureau of the Census

Questions

Documents 1 and 2: "What Is a Ruleville Education?" (1964) and "Mississippi occupations and income by race in 1960."

With your partner(s), read the documents and agree on answers to the following questions. We'll discuss them as class afterward.

1. List three problems mentioned in the first document ("What Is a Ruleville Education?") that were present in Mississippi's segregated schools.

2. How would you describe those same three things in your own school today? How is your school different than those 1960 Mississippi schools? Is there anything that's the same?

3. Look at the tables in the second document ("Mississippi occupations and income by race in 1960"). What kinds of jobs did most Black kids in Mississippi get when they grew up? What kinds of jobs did most white people get? Who made more money, according to the second table?

4. In Mississippi in 1960, nearly every school board member, every elected official, every plantation owner, and every business leader was white. They decided how much money went to segregated schools for Black kids. Do you think they wanted those kids to be uneducated and uninformed? Why or why not?

Document 3: Comments on Milwaukee Schools by Black residents, 1965 (excerpts).

http://wihist.org/1uUxFM6

Black Milwaukee residents made these comments about the city's segregated schools in 1965:

-- Those schools should have been torn down long ago. I work on construction, help build schools -- in other areas they have everything. The lobbys are bigger than the auditoriums around here.

-- The curriculum is not up to date. The textbooks are not what they should be, and the teachers are not in sympathy with the kids.

-- There is so much difference between the Negro and White school children. Kids on the side don't know anything about their subjects; the way they conduct themselves and their environments are different. I was really suprised -- the the kids from this side have to play by themselves.

-- Most of the White schools have first-class facilities whereas, we have to use the things that they don't want anymore.

-- Because they could have lunch rooms and more playground space, more room on the sidewalk and more crossing guards.

-- Some of the teachers are prejudiced.

-- Well, I could say that the teachers are not rough enough on the kids.

-- I feel that Negro children being moved from one area to another is bad. It is unfair to go somewhere where you are not wanted. I also feel that they should have more schools built in Negro neighborhoods and all this trouble could be avoided.

-- Some kids don't get the books that they need. They get the old books from the White schools. I think they should have just what the White schools should have.

Questions

Document 3: Comments on Milwaukee Schools by Black residents, 1965 (excerpts).

With your partner(s), read the comments and make notes on the following questions. We'll discuss them as a class afterward.

1. List three problems that Milwaukee's segregated schools faced in 1964. Were they similar to the problems you listed for Mississippi schools?

2. Who in Milwaukee made the decisions in 1965 about public schools, like allocating money for new buildings, deciding how big classes would be, or what courses were offered, etc.? Do you think they wanted Black kids to be uneducated and uninformed, like the decision makers in Mississippi? Why do you think that?

3. Think of some people you've met who didn't finish high school. Do they have the skills they need to affect their future? How much money do you think they make, compared to occupations that require degrees?

4. Do you think there is a connection between the education students receive and the jobs they get? What choices do you think you should make about school?

Civil Rights: For or Against?

Goals

Students learn how to identify the main point in an informational text, assess the evidence and reasoning behind it, and decide whether to accept or reject it by analyzing at Student Nonviolent Coordinating Committee (SNCC) pamphlet and a Citizen's Council advertisement.

Central Questions

When someone claims something is true, how do you decide whether he or she is right? When you see something in a historical document, on the web, or on television, how do you decide whether or not you should believe it?

Background Information

Today the question of whether or not to support the Civil Rights Movement seems odd, but at that time the issue was not at all clear to millions of Americans. Many white people thought the movement was unnecessary or dangerous. Many African Americans were justifiably afraid that if they joined the movement, they would be punished by authorities or even killed by racist terror groups like the Ku Klux Klan.

The first document in this lesson plan was published by the Citizens' Council in Selma, Alabama. The councils were a sort of white-supremacist Chamber of Commerce; some historians have called them, "the Klan in suits and ties." Business leaders across the South formed the councils in the late 1950s to oppose integration through marketing campaigns and direct action. Members worked together to shape public opinion and to punish Black residents who supported civil rights by firing them from jobs, foreclosing on their mortgages, and more. The full-page newspaper advertisement from 1963 encourages white readers to join the local Citizens' Council and help stop the Civil Rights Movement.

The second document is from a 1964 brochure urging Black Mississippians to support the Freedom Summer volunteers who were planning to enter their communities. It was prepared by the Council of Federated Organizations (COFO), a coalition of major civil rights organizations in Mississippi and the sponsor of Freedom Summer. These two pages are from a six-page mimeographed brochure asking local Black residents to support civil rights workers rather than stand on the sidelines.

Documents Used in This Lesson:

1. "Ask Yourself This Important Question: What Have I Personally Done to Maintain Segregation?"
   http://wihist.org/1vFbVmr
2. Mississippi Freedom Summer brochure (excerpts).
   http://wihist.org/1zlygGi

You may want to copy the two documents back-to-back and the two-page worksheet the same way. Students can then work in pairs or small groups to analyze the documents. Each group of students would need a pair of worksheets (one to analyze each document).

Document 1: Ask Yourself This Important Question: What Have I Personally Done to Maintain Segregation."

http://wihist.org/1vFbVmr

ASK YOURSELF THIS IMPORTANT QUESTION:
What have I personally done to Maintain Segregation?

If the answer disturbs you, probe deeper and decide what you are willing to do to preserve racial harmony in Selma and Dallas County.

Is it worth four dollars to prevent a "Birmingham" here? That's what it costs to be a member of your Citizens Council, whose efforts are not thwarted by courts which give sit-in demonstrators legal immunity, prevent school boards from expelling students who participate in mob activities and would place federal referees at the board of voter registrars.

Law enforcement can be called only after these things occur, but your Citizens Council prevents them from happening.

Why else did only 350 Negroes attend a so-called mass voter registration meeting that outside agitators worked 60 days to organize in Selma?

Gov. Wallace told a state meeting of the council three weeks ago: "You are doing a wonderful job, but you should speak with the united voice of 100,000 persons. Go back home and get more members."

Gov. Wallace stands in the University doorway next Tuesday facing possible ten years imprisonment for violating a federal injunction.

Is it worth four dollars to you to prevent sit-ins, mob marches and wholesale Negro voter registration efforts in Selma?

If so, prove your dedication by joining and supporting the work of the Dallas County Citizens Council today. Six dollars will make both you and your wife members of an organization which has already given Selma nine years of Racial Harmony since "Black Monday."

Send Your Check To
THE DALLAS COUNTY
Citizens Council

SELMA, ALABAMA
YOUR MEMBERSHIP IS GOOD FOR 12 MONTHS

Document 2: Mississippi Freedom Summer brochure (excerpts).

Two panels from a folding brochure addressed to local Black residents of Mississippi by COFO.

The whole brochure is online at http://wihist.org/1zlygGi

Voter Registration

ARE YOU A REGISTERED VOTER?

If we were all voting then things would be better in Mississippi.

We would have:
- enough food
- more jobs
- better schools
- better houses
- paved sidewalks

People coming here this summer can work with you on VOTER REGISTRATION. They can knock on doors, teach the registration forms and drive people to the courthouse. They can help in any way you want them to.

What You Can Do:

This is your FREEDOM SUMMER. It will not work without your help.

COFO is asking you to:
- provide housing for the people who are coming to work here.
- look for buildings which can be used for Freedom Schools and Community Centers.
- get names of students who want to go to Freedom Schools.
- let us know when you have meetings or arrange meetings so we can come answer questions about the FREEDOM SUMMER.

Many people are coming here to work during our FREEDOM SUMMER. They want to learn about Mississippi. They feel that the problems here are the problems of people all over the country. Most of them will be college students, both Negro and white.

COFO is your organization. The things it is trying to do should be done by the state. The people who have been elected to run the state say that they do not have to do things for Negroes.

IT IS THE FAULT OF THE STATE that you cannot:
- find work
- read and write
- send your children to better schools.

If you work with COFO you will be working to get yourself the better conditions you deserve.

Questions

Document analysis: "Ask Yourself This Important Question" and Mississippi Freedom Summer brochure.

With a partner, read the document and try to discover answers to the following questions. You may not be able to find answers to them all.

1. Write the document's title, or make one up that describes it.

2. What kind of document is it (book, letter, advertisement, article, flier, pamphlet, etc.)?

3. When and where was it made?

4. Who created it? Who did they make it for?

5. What is the main point? What is it trying to say? Restate it in your own words.

6. What did the creator assume about the audience?

   a. *Values:* What does the author think is good and bad? What do you think one of the author's unspoken values was?

   b. *Standards:* What did the author think was ideal or best for society? What did he or she think is the opposite of that?

   c. *Biases and prejudices:* Some values and standards are so deeply rooted and basic that authors don't even explain them. Strong statements that aren't backed by evidence often reflect biases. Name one of the author's biases.

7. What evidence does the author give to support his or her main point or assumptions?
   Evidence is facts offered to support the main point. It usually includes a description of the author's personal experience or quotations from authorities with more knowledge or experience. Write down the evidence the author provides to prove the main point. Does the evidence look relevant to the main point? Trustworthy? Complete?

8. Outline the main point, assumptions, and evidence you found in the document this way: assumptions + evidence, therefore main point.

9. Does the argument in the document make sense to you? Do you agree or disagree with the argument? Would you be likely to take the action it recommends? Why?

Neutrality or Engagement?

Goals

Students analyze a political cartoon and a diary entry that highlight the risks taken by civil rights workers in the 1960s. They imagine themselves in similar situations and consider conflicting motivations and responsibilities. Then they evaluate how much they would sacrifice for an ideal.

Central Questions

Many Black Mississippians—including Black ministers, teachers, and business owners—chose not to get involved in the Civil Rights Movement because of the dangers connected with participating. What do you think you would have done when Student Nonviolent Coordinating Committee (SNCC) or Congress of Racial Equality (CORE) came to your town? Was joining the movement worth the risk?

Background Information

Many people willingly put their lives and safety on the line to fight for civil rights. But other people chose not to get involved from fear of being punished by the police, employers, or terrorist groups. The dangers were very real: during the 1964 Freedom Summer, there were at least six murders, 29 shootings, 50 fire-bombings, more than 60 beatings, and over 400 arrests in Mississippi.

Despite their fears, 80,000 residents, mostly African Americans, risked harassment and intimidation to cast ballots in the Freedom Vote of November 1963. But the next year, during 1964's Freedom Summer, only 16,000 black Mississippians tried to register to vote in the official election that fall.

"The people are scared," James Forman of SNCC told a reporter. "They tell us, 'All right. I'll go down to register [to vote], but what you going to do for me when I lose my job and they beat my head?'"

We hear many stories about courage and heroism, but not many about people who didn't dare to get involved. We like to imagine that we would have been one of the heroes. But would we? What does it take to risk everything for an ideal?

Documents Used in This Lesson:

1. Political cartoon, "Caught him trespassin' on private property!" This cartoon by Frank Miller appeared in the *Des Moines Register* on July 10, 1964.
   http://wihist.org/1FOlvWy

2. Walter Kaufmann's diary entry for Aug. 15-16, 1964 (excerpt). Kaufmann describes violent incidents he witnessed during his first two days in Mississippi.
   http://wihist.org/11WzwEJ

Document 1: Political cartoon, "Caught him trespassin' on private property!" This cartoon by Frank Miller appeared in the Des Moines Register on July 10, 1964.
http://wihist.org/1FOlvWy

Questions

Cartoon Analysis: "Caught him trespassin' on private property!"

Work with a partner or small group to answer these questions.

1. Identify the cartoon's caption or title.

2. Record any important dates or numbers that appear in the cartoon.

3. Locate three words or phrases that identify objects or people. Which appear to be the most significant? Why do you think so?

4. List the objects or people you see in the cartoon. Which ones are symbols for an idea?

5. Explain how the words in the cartoon clarify the symbols.

8. List adjectives that describe the emotions portrayed in the cartoon.

9. Explain the main message of the cartoon in your own words.

10. What groups would agree or disagree with the cartoon's message?

Document 2: Walter Kaufmann's diary entry for Aug. 15-16, 1964 (excerpt).
http://wihist.org/11WzwEJ

Date: Sat Aug 15th

ARRIVED JACPSON MISS COFO OFFICE APPROX. 10:30 PM SAT.,
5 MIN. LATER A VOLUNTEER WORKER WEAS ASSAULTED WITH A BASEBALL
BAT DIRECTLY ACROSS THE STREET FROM THE COFO OFFICE. TWELVE
STITCHES WERE TAKEN IN HIS HEAD. THE OFFICE IS IN THE HEART
OF THE NEGRO GHETTO --THE ASSAILANTS WERE WHITE.

TEN MINUTES LATER, SILAS MAGEE, FIELD SECRETARY FOR SNCC,
WAS SHOT IN THE HEAD IN GREENWOOD, MISS., FIVE MIN. LATER, A
NEGRO WAS SHOT IN THE LEG ON LYNCH STREET, ONLY ONE BLOCK FROM
THE OFFICE. SILMUNTANEOUSLY A CROSS WAS BURNED AT TERRY AND
LYNCH STREET,S ONLY FOUR BLOCKS FROM THE COFO OFFICE.

Sun. Aug 16th

LEFT COFO OFFICE 10AM FOR MILESTON, MISS. TO INTERVIEW
HARDIMAN TURNBOLT, AN ELECTED DELEGATE TO THE NATIONAL DEMOCRATIC
CONVENTION FOR THE FREEDOM DEMOCRAT PARTY. HE IS A LIFETIME
RESIDENT OF MISS., SEMI-ILLITERATE BUT A NATURAL LEADER AND A
DYNAMIC PERSONALITY. HE SAYS THAT HE IS FED UP WITH THE TREATMENT
OF THE NEGROES AND JUST CANT TAKE ANY MORE. EARLIER THIS YEAR,
HE LED A GROUP OF 14 NEGROES YO THE COURTHOUSE IN HOLMES COUNTY
TO REGISTER. THE SHERIFF LINED THEM UP, PULLED HIS GUN, AND
ASKED, "WHO WANTS TO BE FIRST?", HARDIMAN TURNBOLT IMMEDIATELY
STEPPED FORWARD AND SAID "ME". THE SHERIFF WAS SO SURPRISED
THAT HE DID NOT SHOOT BUT HOLSTERED HIS PISTOL AND TOLD THEM
ALL TO GO HOME.

2 WEEKS LATER, HIS HOME WAS FIRE-BOMBED, AND AS HE , HIS
WIFE AND TWELVE YEAR OLD DAUGHTER WERE FLEEING THE BURNING BLDG.,
HE WAS FIRED UPON BY WHITES, HE REPELLED THEM BY FIRING BACK,
WHICH HE HAS DONE ON TWO OCCASIONS SINCE THEN.

COFO: Council of Federated Organizations, the coalition that ran Freedom Summer.
SNCC: Student Nonviolent Coordinating Committee, the most active group during Freedom Summer.
"Hardiman Turnbolt" was actually Hartman Turnbow.

Questions

Document 2: Walter Kaufmann's diary entry for Aug. 15-16, 1964 (excerpt).

1. Make the diary your own. Choose one of the two activities below.

Write a story: Retell what happened to Mr. Turnbow as if it happened to you. Imagine you or your family are in that situation and tell the story through your own eyes. Make up any details or ending you want.

or

Make a sketch: Draw something to represent one of the incidents Walter Kaufmann described. What did you find the most interesting, moving, offensive, or powerful? Use your art to represent what happened—and how you felt about it.

2. Values clarification exercise

Take five index cards. Write on each card something that you value a lot: a possession, your job, a person you love, your reputation, your home, your health, a cherished pet, your church, making art or music, a sport that you do, feeling safe in your neighborhood—anything that you value deeply. Write a different thing on each card. Put the five cards aside.

Now write on a piece of paper an issue or a cause that you care about: animal rights, police brutality, the right to vote, women's equality, gay marriage, climate change, homelessness, reproductive rights, or any other issue that you feel strongly about.

Pick up your index cards again. Which valuable thing would you give up to help that cause? Crumble up that index card and throw it in the wastebasket. Which valuable thing would you sacrifice next? Continue until you have only one card left. Would you give that up, too?

List three things people in your grandparents' generation risked or sacrificed in order to secure the right to vote and end racial discrimination. That's why you have all the opportunities that you do today.

Getting the Message Out

Goals

Students learn how Student Nonviolent Coordinating Committee (SNCC) managed the media during the Civil Rights Movement, examine marketing and public relations techniques, examine their own media consumption, and write a press release.

Central Questions

How did Freedom Summer's leaders get their message out? How do organizations do that today? How trustworthy are marketing and PR messages? What can students learn from them about their own communication styles?

Background Information

During the Civil Rights Movement of the 1960s, SNCC used press releases, photographs, television spots, brochures, posters, and direct contact with journalists to teach the nation about the struggle against segregation. SNCC depended upon articulate, charismatic, and savvy leaders like Julian Bond, Diane Nash, Stokely Carmichael, James Forman, and Bob Moses, all of whom worked well with the news media. That media consisted of newspaper reporters who took notes on paper, typed stories on typewriters, and sent them to their papers over the telegraph; there were no laptops or smartphones and no Internet. Television was crude, and cameras were expensive and not very portable. No social media existed.

Mary Elizabeth King worked on SNCC's communication team for four years. Her job involved phoning jails when activists were arrested, calling news media to give them stories about the movement, connecting SNCC offices to pass along news, and publishing SNCC's newspaper, *The Student Voice*. She later wrote a short article (excerpted below) explaining how all this was done.

Today, every organization, business and government agency has a marketing and public relations staff, most of whom are trained in psychology and communications skills. Their job is to make the public believe their messages and feel certain emotions. Their messages compete for our attention 24 hours a day from our TVs, radios, computer screens, phones, and billboards.

SNCC's public relations campaign was a great success and focused the nation's attention on Mississippi for much of 1964. Mainstream Americans were shocked at the injustices they saw, and many of them lobbied their representatives in Washington for reform. When Americans all over the country learned about the segregated South, they changed their thinking about race. This helped pressure Congress to pass the Civil Rights Act in July 1964 and the Voting Rights Act in August 1965.

Documents Used in This Lesson:

1. "How We Made the Media Pay Attention" (excerpt) By Mary Elizabeth King.
   http://wihist.org/1FYapQU
2. "Bombing Won't Halt SNCC Drive," SNCC Press release, from July 9, 1964.
   http://wihist.org/12Gs15A

Document 1: "How We Made the Media Pay Attention" (excerpt) by Mary Elizabeth King.
http://wihist.org/1FYapQU

How we made the media pay attention

MARY ELIZABETH KING | SEPTEMBER 16, 2011

During the U.S. civil rights movement, Julian Bond and I essentially managed a South-wide information system for the Student Nonviolent Coordinating Committee in what we called the "communications shop." Before me, Dorothy Miller Zellner worked with Julian. (She appears to the left of him, at center, in the photograph above.) To show how important was the public-information function to SNCC, Bond held one of the few titles in our egalitarian organization: Press Secretary.

Our work was to get unreported accounts into news media circuits, recount unfolding stories, and ease the difficulties of working journalists who were trying to cover a complex mobilization. An additional purpose was to provide protection for civil rights workers. A reporter appearing at a jailhouse with pen and pad in hand might be the only intervention that could save the life of an arrested volunteer or staff member, because the sheriff or police would know that with a published news account that an individual was behind bars, they could no longer operate with impunity. The flow of information from our communications office—sharing background and facts from our projects across the southern states—often made it into the regional and national press, and was as significant to our larger objectives such as the organizing of voter registration drives, mounting demonstrations, devising mock ballots, and building alternative political parties.

For the procedures that we created to work, our communications office had to earn credibility as a trustworthy source in the eyes of the national and sometimes international news corps. The reporters, whom we came know personally, were sometimes indifferent, rushing to meet deadlines, or suspicious of being exploited by propagandists. Julian's natural inclination toward understatement set the tone. We avoided sensationalism, underestimated the numbers of individuals participating in movement activities, and triple-verified any count of atrocities. Even then, we might undercount in order to be safe. We attributed facts to named sources. The style was clear and unembellished with no opinions or value judgments.

Questions

Document 1: "How We Made the Media Pay Attention" (excerpt) by Mary Elizabeth King.

With a partner, read "How We Made the Media Pay Attention." Agree on answers to the following questions.

1. What does King say was the most important goal for her office? How did they achieve it?

2. Every organization, business, and government agency has people doing work like Mary King describes. List three skills communications workers need to have. Where do people get those skills?

3. Public relations professionals are paid to make us believe and feel certain feelings so that we will act in ways that benefit them. Can you think of an information source that's not biased in this way?

4. Where do you get your news about the world? Who decides what you should know about and what you should think about it? List three sources you read or watch. How do you tell if a source is trustworthy?

Document 2: "Bombing Won't Halt SNCC Drive" press release, July 9, 1964.
http://cdm15932.contentdm.oclc.org/cdm/ref/collection/p15932coll2/id/24249

NEWS RELEASE   # 61
STUDENT NONVIOLENT COORDINATING COMMITTEE   FOR IMMEDIATE RELEASE
6 RAYMOND STREET, N.W.   July 9, 1964
ATLANTA, GEORGIA 30314

                    BOMBING WON'T HALT SNCC DRIVE

McCOMB, MISSISSIPPI - Despite three dynamite blasts that rocked a Negro

home here July 8 and a history of violence, a Student Nonviolent Coor-

dinating Committee (SNCC) voting and educational project will continue.

     Ten voter registration workers in the home at 702 Wall Street here

were not seriously injured. One, Curtis Hayes, 22, a SNCC worker, was

cut by flying glass. Another, SNCC Mississippi Summer Project Volun-

teer Dennis Sweeny, 21, of Portland, Oregon, suffered a mild concussion.

     Others in the home were SNCC workers George and Freddye Greene,
20 and 19, both from Greenwood, Mississippi; SNCC worker Julius Sam-
stein, 25, of New York City; SNCC worker Jesse Harris, 22, of Jackson,
Mississippi; SNCC worker Sherry Everitt, 19, from Pittsburgh, Pa.; CORE
worker Pat Walker, from New York City; and summer volunteers Don McCord,
26, of Stafford, Kansas and Clinton Hopson, 26, of Asbury Park, New
Jersey.

     Samstein, Sweeney, McCord, and Walker are white; the others are
Negroes.

     Three Negro homes were bombed in McComb on June 23. This small
southwest Mississippi town was the site of the first Student Nonviolent
Coordinating Committee voter registration project in 1961. SNCC worker
Bob Moses, now Program Director for the state-wide Mississippi Freedom
Summer Project, began work as the first SNCC field worker in August,
1961.
     The drive three years ago was met with official resistance and ter-
ror tactics from local whites, as is the state-wide drive today.
     Moses and other SNCC staff members, including Hayes, who joined
the anti-segregation group's staff then, were jailed several times by
local law officers. Moses was jailed in nearby Liberty on August 15,
1961, as he accompanied three people to the registrar's office there.
On August 29, 1961, he was beaten by the son of Mississippi law officer
on a Liberty street.
     A local Negro supporter, Herbert Lee, was killed September 25,
1961, by a member of the state legislature, and a witness to that shoot-
ing was murdered on February 1, 1964.
     The Ku Klux Klan and another racist group, the Americans for Pre-
servation of the White Race (APWR) have begun organizational drives
throughout Southwest Mississippi. Arsene Dick, APWR president, says
his all-male, all-white group has chapters in 30 Mississippi counties
and a membership "in the five figure bracket."
     There are more than 15,000 Negroes in Pike County. Fewer than
164 are registered voters.

     SNCC now has voter registration workers in each of Mississippi's
five Congressional Districts.
                              -30-

Questions

Document 2: SNCC Press release, "Bombing Won't Halt SNCC Drive," July 9, 1964.

Write a press release following the format of the SNCC document about an event that you have witnessed. It could be a basketball game you attended, a car accident you saw in the street, a new policy announced by your school, or anything else that actually happened in your community. Imagine that your press release will be posted on a website or printed in a newspaper.

The questions below will help you gather and arrange the facts before you begin. These are the questions reporters try to answer before they tell a story. Limit your press release to 350 words.

1. What are you describing? Use two or three words: a "public meeting," a "soccer game."

2. Who is your target audience? Who are you trying to reach?

3. What's the main point you want people to remember after reading your press release?

4. Where did it happen? Be specific.

5. When did it happen? Be precise.

6. Who were the principal people involved? How are their names spelled? What roles did they play?

7. What is your attention-getting first sentence?

8. What happened? How and why?

The Power of Freedom Schools

Goals

Students compare two 1964 textbook excerpts about Black history, analyze a photograph, and draw conclusions about the value of good schools.

Central Questions

In many segregated Mississippi schools, Black students were taught that white leaders had always treated African Americans kindly. Freedom Schools offered a different perspective on Black history and encouraged critical thinking. What were the consequences of these different educational messages?

Background Information

In 1960, almost half of Mississippi's residents were African American. Two-thirds worked as field hands or as servants. Most had less than a sixth-grade education, and thousands could not read or write.

From the governor's office to the pulpit, in the classroom and the media, virtually every authority figure taught that Black people were inferior to whites and had to be kept in submission. Many people accepted white-supremacist propaganda as common sense. After decades of this indoctrination, most whites believed segregation was necessary. Most African Americans limited their hopes and dreams.

Segregated schools designed by racist administrators created two generations of uninformed Black Mississippians. The best example of this is the comment made by one elderly resident to a Freedom Summer volunteer: "I didn't know colored people could vote." If knowledge is power, then ignorance is powerlessness.

The Freedom Schools started during the 1964 Mississippi summer project were a deliberate attempt to undermine this indoctrination by teaching accurate history and encouraging critical thinking. Charles Cobb, who originated the Freedom Schools idea, argued that "to encourage questions is to encourage challenge, which is to encourage overthrow."

Cobb was right. At the end of the summer, the coordinator of the program remarked that students "began to discover that they themselves could take action against the injustices which kept them unhappy and impotent … Through the study of Negro history they began to have a sense of themselves as a people who could produce heroes."

Documents Used in This Lesson:

1. Excerpt from a Mississippi textbook for segregated elementary schools.
   http://wihist.org/1CmRgrW
2. "What Slavery Was Like" (excerpt from the Freedom School curriculum on Black history).
   http://wihist.org/1I5oOwr
3. "I Didn't Know Colored People Could Vote" Photograph from *The Student Voice*, May 26, 1964.
   http://wihist.org/1vRcfyn

Document 1: Excerpt from a Mississippi textbook for segregated elementary schools.
http://wihist.org/1CmRgrW

God wanted the white people to live alone. And he wanted colored people to live alone. The white men built America for you. White people built America so they could make the rules. George Washington was a brave and honest white man. The white men cut away big forests. The white man has always been kind to the Negro. We do not believe that God wants us to live together. Negro people like to live by themselves. Negroes use their own bathrooms. They do not use white people's bathrooms. The Negro has his own part of town to live in. This is called our Southern Way of Life. Do you know that some people want the Negroes to live with white people? These people want us to be unhappy. They say we must go to school together. They say we must swim together and use the bathroom together. God had made us different. And God knows best. Did you know that our country will grow weak if we mix the races? White men worked hard to build our country. We want to keep it strong and free.

Document 2: "What Slavery Was Like" (excerpt from a Freedom School textbook, 1964).
http://wihist.org/1I5oOwr

What Slavery Was Like

Perhaps the simplest way to understand what slavery was like is to read the accounts of slaves who survived to tell about it: Frederick Douglass, Harriet Tubman, Booker T. Washington. All three lived in the Upper South (Maryland and Virginia). In the Deep South conditions were worse.

They were always hungry. On the plantation where Douglass grew up, the children were often fed scraps in a trough. Frederick recalled fighting with the dog for food. Booker Washington never remembered his family sitting down to dinner together before emancipation. Harriet Tubman was once nearly killed for stealing a lump of sugar.

Clothing was scanty. Children wore a one piece garment, a long shirt. It was made of so rough a material, Washington recalled, that it was torture to "break in" a new shirt.

Booker Washington never slept in a bed until emancipation. Douglass often slept with his head in a sack to keep out the cold, his feet sometimes splitting from frost. Harriet Tubman sometimes slept with her feet in the ashes of the fire.

Douglass saw his Aunt Esther get forty lashes. He saw a cousin walk onto his plantation from a plantation twelve miles distant, covered with blood from a beating; she was ordered to go back home. Harriet Tubman was hit in the head by a piece of iron thrown by an overseer, and suffered from dizzy spells for the rest of her life.

Questions

Documents 1 and 2: Excerpt from a Mississippi textbook for segregated schools and "What Slavery Was Like" from a Freedom School textbook.

With a partner, agree on answers to these questions.

1. In the first document, what message do Black children get about US history and race relations? What evidence does the author give that this view is right? Who does he or she appeal to as an authority? What did the author want students to think or do?

2. How is the version of history in the second excerpt different from the first? What evidence does the author give to support these views? Who does he or she appeal to as an authority? What does the author want students to think or do?

3. Which of the two textbooks do you think is more trustworthy and accurate? Why do you think that?

4. What could happen to kids whose only sources of information were biased and incomplete?

Document 3: "I Didn't Know Colored People Could Vote" *The Student Voice*, May 26, 1964.
http://wihist.org/1vRcfyn

'I didn't know colored people could vote.'

"I came up on a porch and an ancient man says "Yes, sir" and offers me his chair. An enraged white face shouts curses out of a car window. We are greeted with fear at the door: "I didn't know colored people could vote." And people ask why we are down here . . . ."

– from a white SNCC worker's field report.

Questions

Document 3: "I Didn't Know Colored People Could Vote," *The Student Voice*, May 26, 1964.

1. Is the man in the photo rich, middle-class, or poor? What clues in the picture support your answer?

2. This man only went to segregated schools that used textbooks like the first one quoted in document 1. His comment reveals one effect of being educated in bad schools. List three other consequences.

3. Which Mississippians benefited if many African American kids grew up to be as uninformed as this old man? Who profits today if Americans are kept uninformed about the world?

4. List some of the messages about the United States you got from the textbooks you've used over the years. What are some things you assume or take for granted about your country?

PART THREE

Lessons about Pivotal Events and Issues in Civil Rights History

Brown v. Board of Education (1954)

Goals

Students learn about the pivotal 1954 *Brown v. Board of Education* case by watching a PBS video, reading excerpts from the decision, and analyzing a political cartoon. They debate the proper role of government in community affairs and citizens' lives.

Central Questions

Why was this case brought to the Supreme Court? What are the proper roles for federal, state and local governments?

Background Information

In 1868, the 14th Amendment to the Constitution guaranteed equal protection under the laws to everyone, regardless of race. In 1896, the Supreme Court said in the case of *Plessy v. Ferguson* that racial segregation was legal as long as facilities for Blacks and whites were "separate but equal." In the early 1950s, the NAACP brought five lawsuits in Kansas, South Carolina, Virginia, the District of Columbia, and Delaware claiming that the "separate but equal" ruling violated the equal protection clause of the 14th Amendment. All of the lawsuits concerned segregated schools and the equal right to education.

In 1952, the five cases reached the Supreme Court, which agreed to hear all of them as one. Thurgood Marshall, a lead attorney for the National Association for the Advancement of Colored People (NAACP), provided testimony from more than 30 social scientists affirming the harmful effects of segregation on Blacks and whites. On the other side, lawyers for the school boards said that *Plessy v. Ferguson* was more important than the 14th Amendment and they argued that running schools is a local matter and not the business of the federal government.

On May 17, 1954, Chief Justice Earl Warren read the court's unanimous opinion: school segregation was unconstitutional. But desegregating thousands of schools all over the country was a huge challenge, and the court merely said that it had to be done "with all deliberate speed." That phrase allowed many years of foot-dragging by opponents of integration all across the country. The Milwaukee school board, for example, did not come up with a desegregation plan until 1979, 25 years after *Brown v. Board*.

Despite two unanimous decisions, there was widespread resistance to the Supreme Court's ruling, not only among Southern segregationists but also from some constitutional scholars who felt that the court had overstepped its constitutional powers by creating new law. Participants in the Civil Rights Movement, however, believed the court had acted appropriately and used its power to enforce the constitution.

Documents Used in This Lesson:

1. Seven-minute PBS video "Brown: A Landmark Case."
   http://wihist.org/1yAfJYt
2. Excerpts from the Supreme Court's 1954 decision.
   http://wihist.org/1q6K3bx
3. Editorial cartoon: "I'm eight. I was born on the day of the Supreme Court decision."
   http://wihist.org/1yWbHZo

Document 1: Seven-minute PBS video "Brown: A Landmark Case."
http://wihist.org/1yAfJYt

Document 2: Excerpts from the Supreme Court's 1954 decision. http://wihist.org/1q6K3bx

A. "Does segregation of children in public schools solely on the basis of race, even though the physical facilities and other 'tangible' factors may be equal, deprive the children of the minority group of equal educational opportunities? We believe that it does."

B. "Segregation of white and colored children in public schools has a detrimental effect upon the colored children. The impact is greater when it has the sanction of the law, for the policy of separating the races is usually interpreted as denoting the inferiority of the Negro group. A sense of inferiority affects the motivation of a child to learn. Segregation with the sanction of law, therefore, has a tendency to [retard] the educational and mental development of Negro children and to deprive them of some of the benefits they would receive in a racial[ly] integrated school system."

C. "We conclude that, in the field of public education, the doctrine of 'separate but equal' has no place. Separate educational facilities are inherently unequal."

D. In a 1955 follow-up ruling, the Supreme Court ordered state and local officials to "take such proceedings and enter such orders and decrees consistent with this opinion as are necessary and proper to admit [children] to public schools on a racially nondiscriminatory basis with all deliberate speed..."

Questions

Document 1: Seven-minute PBS video " Brown: A Landmark Case."

Before starting, jot down three things that you think will be in the video. Then watch the entire video, making a few notes on things that seem important as you watch it.

1. Surprise – Realize – Visualize

Fold a sheet of paper into thirds. In the left-hand column, list some things that *surprised* you while you were watching. In the middle column, write at least one thing you *realized* while watching, something that you didn't know before. In the right-hand column, *imagine* one thing you might do, or not do, because of watching the video.

Document 2: Excerpts from the Supreme Court's 1954 decision.

1. With a partner or in a group, read the excerpts from the Supreme Court's decision. Select any one of the paragraphs and agree among yourselves on what it means. Restate it briefly in your own words, in a way that somebody younger than you could understand.

2. Opponents of *Brown v. Board of Education* argued that the federal government should not get involved local matters, such as how schools are run. Agree on these questions among yourselves: Should a higher level of government ever be able to overrule a lower one, like a town or a village? On what sorts of issues? Should any government ever be able to take away an individual person's freedom? When?

Document 3: Editorial cartoon: "I'm eight. I was born on the day of the Supreme Court decision."
http://wihist.org/1yWbHZo

Questions

Document 3: Editorial cartoon: "I'm eight. I was born on the day of the Supreme Court decision."

With a partner or in a small group, answer the following questions.

1. What's the cartoon's caption or title?

2. What year was the cartoon published? How long after *Brown v. Board of Education* was that?

3. Who are the main characters? Where are they?

4. List several objects you see in the cartoon. What's going on in the background?

5. Which of the objects on your list are symbols?

6. What do you think each symbol means?

7. Explain the main message of the cartoon in your own words.

8. Think of a message about something going on now in the world, your neighborhood, or your school. Make a rough sketch of a cartoon that would illustrate your message.

Civil Rights Act of 1964

Goals

By rephrasing two paragraphs from the act and analyzing a photo and an advertisement, students will learn about its main provisions and why those were considered controversial in 1964. Activities challenge them to take a side in the conflict between civil rights and property rights and explain their stance.

Central Questions

What did the Civil Rights Act of 1964 say and do? Why did some people oppose it?

Background Information

Congress had passed various civil right bills for almost a century before the Civil Rights Act of 1964. All the bills aimed to articulate and guarantee rights that were outlined in the 14th and 15th amendments to the Constitution. These passed just after the Civil War and aimed to ensure equal protection under the law and protect the right to vote for African Americans. They generally failed because they had loopholes and enforcement was left to state and local officials.

After the federal government abandoned the South in 1877, many states all over the country passed explicitly segregationist laws. In 1896, the US Supreme Court held up these laws in its *Plessy v. Ferguson* decision. For decades, millions of African Americans were denied their basic civil rights.

Following World War II, Congress passed bills desegregating the military and interstate transportation. In 1954, the Supreme Court's unanimous *Brown v. Board of Education* decision overturned segregation in public schools. The much-publicized Montgomery bus boycott in Alabama launched Martin Luther King Jr. to national prominence, and the use of federal troops to desegregate Little Rock's Central High School in 1957 demonstrated a revival of federal interest in civil rights.

Progress was slow, however, and during the early 1960s, the Council of Racial Equality (CORE) and the Student Nonviolent Coordinating Committee (SNCC) organized hundreds of sit-ins and other direct actions. Photos revealing inequality and violence flooded the news media.

In a televised address on June 11, 1963, President John F. Kennedy Jr. proposed a new and more explicit civil rights bill. After Kennedy's assassination, President Lyndon B. Johnson continued to lobby for the bill in Congress, where a cohort of key segregationist senators from the South filibustered for 75 days to stop it. They relented in June 1964, at the start of Freedom Summer, and Johnson ultimately signed it into law on July 2, 1964. Although strengthened and supplemented in subsequent years, the Civil Rights Act of 1964 officially made racial discrimination and segregation illegal.

Documents Used in This Lesson:

1. Civil Rights Act of 1964, July 2, 1964 (excerpts).
   http://wihist.org/1wK5oK4
2. Restaurant owner Lester Maddox drives away black customer at gunpoint.
   http://wihist.org/1yATFNk
3. "$100 Billion Blackjack."
   http://wihist.org/1OjkIUA

Questions

Document 1: Excerpts from the Civil Rights Act of 1964.

With a partner, restate each paragraph from the act in a short sentence of your own:

SEC. 201. (a) All persons shall be entitled to the full and equal enjoyment of the goods, services, facilities, and privileges, advantages, and accommodations of any place of public accommodation, as defined in this section, without discrimination or segregation on the ground of race, color, religion, or national origin… [such as] any inn, hotel, motel, … any restaurant, cafeteria, lunchroom, lunch counter, soda fountain… any motion picture house, theater, concert hall, sports arena, stadium…

SEC. 202. All persons shall be entitled to be free, at any establishment or place, from discrimination or segregation of any kind on the ground of race, color, religion, or national origin, [even] if such discrimination or segregation is or purports to be required by any law, statute, ordinance...

Document 2: Restaurant owner Lester Maddox drives a Black customer away at gunpoint.

If you can decide who gets to borrow your phone or your jacket, why can't he decide who to serve in his restaurant? What are some differences between these two situations?

Document 3: "$100 Billion Blackjack."
http://wihist.org/1OjkIUA

This flier was distributed by mail and as a newspaper ad during the spring of 1964. Don't try to read the small print. Just focus on the big type that you can make out easily.

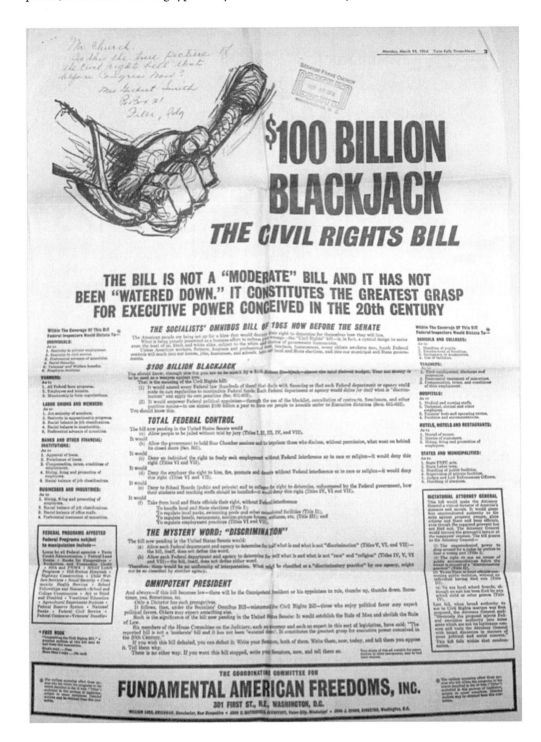

Questions

Document 3: "$100 Billion Blackjack," spring 1964.

In a small group, agree on answers to the following questions. Don't try to read the small print. Just focus on the big type that you can make out easily.

1. Who produced and distributed this advertisement?

2. Were they for or against the Civil Rights Act? What images or words tell you that?

3. What's their main argument? Restate it in a phrase or sentence of your own.

4. Do you agree or disagree with their main point? Explain why.

5. Do you think the constitutional argument against civil rights may have just been a cover for racism? Why or why not?

The Voting Rights Act of 1965

Goals

By analyzing first-person accounts from Mississippi, students discover why the act was needed and learn how literacy tests, harassment, and violence disenfranchised Black residents. They then analyze key provisions of the act and examine challenges to voting rights in the United States today.

Central Questions

Why was the law necessary? Why hadn't most African Americans registered and voted in the South before 1965? What does the law say? How did it change voting patterns?

Background information

The 14th and 15th amendments to the Constitution, passed just after the Civil War, tried to ensure equal protection under the law and protect the right to vote for African Americans. After the federal government abandoned the South in 1877, many states passed explicit segregationist laws. In 1896, the US Supreme Court upheld these laws in its *Plessy v. Ferguson* decision. For decades, millions of African Americans were denied their basic civil rights all across the United States, including the right to vote.

Literacy tests, poll taxes (taxes that essentially charged a fee for voting), harassment, and terrorist attacks discouraged Black residents from registering to vote. In Mississippi, all the people who tried to register had their names published in the local newspaper for two weeks. Black residents often found themselves evicted from their homes, fired from their jobs, and threatened with violence after they attempted to register. Those who tried to organize voters or teach voter education classes were sometimes arrested, tortured, or driven out of the state. By 1960, more than 90 percent of eligible Black voters in Mississippi were not registered, even in counties where African Americans were a majority.

In 1964, Congress passed a new Civil Rights Act with a section guaranteeing the right to vote, but it had no provision for the federal government to enforce it and was widely ignored. After the murder of three Freedom Summer workers in June 1964 and television coverage of unprovoked attacks on marchers in Selma, Alabama, in March 1965, Congress finally passed the Voting Rights Act. It outlawed poll taxes and literacy tests, and explicitly gave federal officials power to occupy local courthouses and take over registration in counties that showed a pattern of discrimination.

Within 18 months, the majority of eligible Black voters in the South had registered. Many ran for local office, and both national political parties began to see African Americans as an important constituency.

Documents Used in This Lesson:

1. Violence against Black Mississippi residents who tried to vote, 1963-1964 (from sworn affidavits in a legal case that led up to the act.)
   http://wihist.org/1w0WuWU
2. A Freedom Summer worker describes Mississippi's voter test, 1964.
   http://wihist.org/12wQyt2
3. Voting Rights Act of 1965 (excerpts).
   http://wihist.org/1vzUWn8

Document 1: Violence against Black Mississippi residents who tried to vote, 1963-1964 (from sworn affidavits in a legal case that led up to the act).

http://wihist.org/1w0WuWU

June 9, 1963: Fannie Lou Hamer and five other registration workers were arrested in Winona on their way home from a registration workshop in Charleston, S.C. They were held in the Winona jail for four days during which time they were severely beaten with nightsticks and fists by policemen and with leather straps by prison trustees under the direction of police officers.

October 30, 1963: A voter registration worker was arrested by Clarksdale police who slugged him and broke his glasses as he was being taken to jail.

November 2, 1963: Three shots were fired at a voter registration worker in Tate County as he drove away from a Freedom Vote poll site.

April 1, 1964: A Negro making his fifth attempt to register to vote in Greenwood was told by a white official to go home before he was arrested. As he was leaving the courthouse, a policeman told him "If I catch you in that line, I will shoot your damn head off."

Document 2: A Freedom Summer worker describes Mississippi's voter test, 1964.

http://wihist.org/12wQyt2

In Mississippi one must fill out a form with 18 questions on it to get on the voting rolls. The 18th question is the kicker. It asks the applicant to read any section of the state constitution the registrar chooses and then to interpret it in simple language to the satisfaction of the registrar. Of course no Negro can satisfy him. We were told that he would sometimes add questions such as, "How many bubbles in a bar of soap?" And he would disqualify anyone for the least error such as putting "M" instead of "Male" on the form. Also, any applicant has his name published in the paper which allows his employer to fire him or informs the local toughs where to lob their bombs.

Questions

Document 1: Violence against Black Mississippi residents who tried to vote, 1963-1964.

1. Read the accounts of what happened to people who tried to register to vote. Who was trying to stop them? Why do you think those people acted the way that they did?

2. What surprised you in those four stories? What did you realize that you hadn't known before?

3. You will be 18 soon (if you're not already). Do you plan to vote in local and national elections? Would you register to vote if you thought someone might treat you the way the people in the four affidavits were treated?

Document 2: A Freedom Summer worker describes the Mississippi voter test, 1964.

1. Could you have passed the Mississippi voter test? Restate this section of the Wisconsin Constitution in your own words: "The members of the assembly shall be chosen biennially, by single districts, on the Tuesday succeeding the first Monday of November in even-numbered years, by the qualified electors of the several districts, such districts to be bounded by county, precinct, town or ward lines, to consist of contiguous territory and be in as compact form as practicable." Assume the person judging your answer wants you to fail.

2. Some Black Mississippi residents took the test several times, as they repeatedly tried to register. What qualities must they have possessed? List five adjectives that describe someone who refused to be scared away.

Document 3: The Voting Rights Act of 1965 (excerpts).

SEC. 2. No voting qualification or prerequisite to voting, or standard, practice, or procedure shall be imposed or applied by any State or political subdivision to deny or abridge the right of any citizen of the United States to vote on account of race or color.

SEC. 3. (a) Whenever the Attorney General institutes a proceeding under any statute to enforce the guarantees of the fifteenth amendment in any State or political subdivision, the court shall authorize the appointment of Federal examiners by the United States Civil Service Commission in accordance with section 6 to serve for such period of time and for such political subdivisions as the court shall determine is appropriate to enforce the guarantees of the fifteenth amendment.

SEC. 4. (a) To assure that the right of citizens of the United States to vote is not denied or abridged on account of race or color, no citizen shall be denied the right to vote in any Federal, State, or local election because of his failure to comply with any test or device in any State…

Questions

Document 3: The Voting Rights Act of 1965 (excerpts).

1. Rephrase each paragraph in your own words. What does each one mean, in a short sentence or phrase?

   Sec. 2:

   Sec. 3:

   Sec. 4:

2. Some people argue that the Voting Rights Act of 1965 is no longer needed because times have changed. What do you think would happen if there were no federal law guaranteeing the right to vote?

3. Other people claim that the law is too broad, and that voters should have to have a state-issued photo ID, like a driver's license. Their opponents point out that many people who are poor and live in large cities don't have cars or driver's licenses, and that getting them is a hardship. Since many of those people are also African American, opponents see the ID requirement as exactly the sort of "prerequisite to voting, or standard, practice, or procedure" that the law prohibits.

   What do you think? Should every voter need a government-issued photo ID? Why or why not? Does requiring one violate the 1965 law? Explain your answers.

Rights in Conflict

Goals

Students gain a greater understanding of the relations between federal authority, local control, property rights, and civil rights, and clarify their beliefs about the role of government.

Central Questions

When, if ever, should the authority of the US government in Washington overrule the right of local people to decide how they live?

Background Information

Government-sponsored segregation was dismantled by a series of court cases culminating in the Civil Rights Act of 1964. The 1954 Supreme Court ruling in *Brown v. Board* made segregated schools illegal, and in 1957 federal troops went into Little Rock, Arkansas, to make sure Black students were allowed to enroll in the city's best high school. In 1963, federal troops were called out again to force the University of Mississippi to open its doors to African Americans.

State leaders like Mississippi governor Ross Barnett argued that they had the right to run their states however they saw fit, including maintaining segregation. Cities and towns, likewise, argued that they had the freedom to run schools, libraries, and other programs any way their voters wanted. Southern leaders publicly urged citizens to disobey the federal civil rights laws.

Beside the issue of states' rights, segregationists also believed that business owners had the freedom to decide who they served in their stores and restaurants. They considered those places to be private property and thought the federal laws were an attack on personal property rights. Some also believed that the federal government had taken away their individual rights as private citizens.

Lawmakers in Washington insisted that the US Constitution guaranteed all Americans certain basic civil rights, and that these took priority over local laws that varied from place to place. But they did little or nothing to enforce the new laws. Officials of the US Justice Department asserted that law enforcement was the responsibility of local police and sheriffs, and usually refused to get involved when civil rights workers were harassed. Black residents and civil rights activists technically had the legal protection of the new laws, but they lived under the constant threat of harassment from local police and violence from white-supremacist groups.

Documents Used in This Lesson:

1. Excerpts from the 14th Amendment, *Brown v. Board* (1954), and the Civil Rights Act of 1964
   http://ourdocuments.gov/
2. Excerpt from a speech by Mississippi Governor Ross R. Barnett, March 7, 1960.
   http://wihist.org/1ACEEtx
3. *Klan Ledger:* An Official Publication of the White Knights of the Ku Klux Klan of Mississippi, Sept. 1964.
   http://wihist.org/1Bo2Sem

Questions

Document 1: Excerpts from the 14th Amendment, *Brown v. Board* (1954) and Civil Rights Act of 1964.

With a partner, read each of these quotations and rewrite its main point in a short sentence or phrase that somebody younger than you could understand.

1868, 14th Amendment: "No State shall make or enforce any law which shall abridge the privileges or immunities of citizens of the United States; nor shall any State deprive any person of life, liberty, or property, without due process of law; nor deny to any person within its jurisdiction the equal protection of the laws."

1954 *Brown v. Board of Education* ruling: "Segregation of white and colored children in public schools has a detrimental effect upon the colored children … We conclude that, in the field of public education, the doctrine of 'separate but equal' has no place. Separate educational facilities are inherently unequal."

1964 Civil Rights Act: "All persons shall be entitled to the full and equal enjoyment of the goods, services, facilities, and privileges, advantages, and accommodations of any place of public accommodation, as defined in this section, without discrimination or segregation on the ground of race, color, religion, or national origin… No person shall withhold, deny, or attempt to withhold or deny, or deprive or attempt to deprive, any person of any right or privilege secured by [this act]…"

Document 2: Excerpt from a speech by Mississippi Governor Ross R. Barnett, March 7, 1960.
http://wihist.org/1ACEEtx

Gov. Barnett was a firm segregationist and states' rights advocate. He helped run the Mississippi Sovereignty Commission, a state agency that fought against the Civil Rights Movement. Barnett gave this speech in New Orleans to a regional meeting of Citizens' Councils, a sort of segregationist Chamber of Commerce. They printed it as a pamphlet, including their two logos shown below.

there are those in our National Government who would once again place New Orleans and the entire South at the mercy of the NAACP and other modern-day Carpetbaggers. At this very moment, our Southern leaders in Congress are battling heroically against vicious Force Bills which would destroy individual freedom.

A willful group of evil men are behind these Force Bills. They would trade the individual freedom and the racial integrity of the South for a few thousand left wing votes in big Northern cities. They have enlisted the aid of powerful and wealthy organizations and are waging constant propaganda warfare against us.

The law which created the Mississippi State Sovereignty Commission stated the Commission's functions in this manner:

"It shall be the duty of the Commission to do and perform any and all acts and things deemed necessary and proper to protect the sovereignty of the State of Mississippi, and her sister states, from encroachment thereon by the Federal Government or any branch, department or agency thereof, and to resist the usurpation of the rights and powers reserved to this state and our sister states by the Federal Government or any branch, department or agency thereof."

Document 3: *Klan Ledger*: An Official Publication of the White Knights of the Ku Klux Klan of Mississippi, Sept. 1964.

http://wihist.org/1Bo2Sem

Tyranny, Treachery, Trickery, Treason is the order of the day in Washington, D.C. Honor, Integrity, Race, Country, America's Christian Religion, are becoming out moded.

Your most precious blood bought individual Freedom --- of choice, of association, of individual independence, of free speech and free press, of control over your children's welfare, of the sacredness of your home and private property, right to run your own business --- of the "right to be let alone by Government", ALL ARE being insidiously but surely eroded and usurped by your overpaid public SERVANTS in an all-powerful central government. Your national Sovereignty and Security have been bartered away by these same U.N. (Not U.S.) public servants. More and more you become a regimental number in a Socialist-Communist Dictatorship. Satan and Antichrist stalk the land. American citizens once were CONSTITUTIONALLY masters, of their Government, including the courts --- but not now.

Questions

Documents 2 and 3: Excerpt from a speech by Mississippi Governor Ross R. Barnett, March 7, 1960 and *Klan Ledger.*

1. Who did the governor consider his enemy?

2. Who did the governor think should control whether a state could practice segregation?

3. In your own words, restate the governor's main message in a single short sentence that somebody younger than you could understand.

4. Who are the people in the first logo symbols for? What's happening there?

5. Use different words to state the mission of the Citizen's Council, as shown in the second logo.

6. What did the Ku Klux Klan writer think was threatened by the federal government in Washington?

7. Which authorities did the Ku Klux Klan writer appeal to?

8. What's the proper role for government?

Put a check mark under each branch of government (or none) that you think should be able to do the thing listed in the first column. You can check more than one column. When you're done, total up each column.

Which level of government should be able to...	federal	state	local	none
start a war with other countries				
decide who gets to vote				
draft people into the military				
collect taxes from people				
allow or prohibit abortions				
decide bus routes and fares				
make people buy pet insurance				
allow or prohibit discrimination by race				
decide highway speed limits				
allow or prohibit marijuana				
decide which neighborhood people can live in				
arrest people for violent crimes				
censor what people write on the web				
decide the drinking age				
make people buy car insurance				
allow or prohibit gun ownership				
decide how much people pay in taxes				
decide what gets shown on television				
spy on people they think are terrorists				
decide what church you go to				
make people buy health insurance				
make people pay their debts				
spy on everyone in order to identify terrorists				
allow or prohibit gay marriage				
decide the price of groceries				
decide what the minimum wage is				
decide what's taught in your school				
Totals:				

In a short sentence, write your opinion of the proper role of each level of government:
("Local government should be the only one who can..." "The federal government should be able to...")

Look at the rows you where you checked "none." Write a single sentence summarizing the parts of life that you think *all* government should stay out of.

Inventing Common Sense

Goals

Students examine a 1964 *New York Times* article quoting white Mississippi residents on race relations, compare Black residents' responses, and dissect an argument about the power of the media. Then they analyze their own media consumption.

Central Questions

In the segregated South, teachers, politicians, newspapers, magazines, television, and radio all taught Black people that they were not as good as white people. How did they do it? What were the consequences? Who is telling us what's important in life? How should we respond?

Background Information

In 1960, almost half of Mississippi's residents were African American. State law kept them apart from whites in neighborhoods, schools, and jobs. Leaders made sure that Black people had the lowest wages, poorest houses, and harshest lives. And most people accepted this as normal, or at least inevitable.

From the governor's office to the pulpit, in the classroom and the media, virtually every authority figure in Mississippi insisted that Black people were dangerous and inferior to whites and had to be kept in submission. After decades of this indoctrination, most whites believed segregation was necessary. Many Blacks had internalized the constant message that they were second-class citizens, limiting their hopes and dreams. White-supremacist propaganda was accepted as common sense. Overt racism that would outrage us today was considered normal.

In Philadelphia, Mississippi, one white minister said, "A minority has taken over the guidance of thought patterns of our town. It has controlled what was said and what was not said." Another resident admitted, "I can understand now how Nazi Germany could grow, with the good people of Germany knowing more of the atrocities than they would admit—and looking away, always looking away. . . . We have been coerced and intimidated."

Changing Jim Crow laws and braving Klan terror attacks were not enough to secure basic human rights. Mississippi residents, white and Black, had to question everything they'd been taught and forge new ideas about people and society. To change the world, they had to change their minds.

Documents Used in This Lesson:

1. "Rights Workers Embitter Delta." New York Times, July 19, 1964 (excerpts).
   http://wihist.org/1u7qew0
2. Residents respond to "Rights Workers Embitter Delta" (excerpts).
   http://wihist.org/1yrhrg7
3. Cobb, Charles E. "Some Notes on Education" (excerpts).
   http://wihist.org/1yrhvfQ

For analysis of students' own media consumption, you might also incorporate some of the tools at Ithaca College's "Project Look Sharp."
http://www.ithaca.edu/looksharp/

Document 1: "Rights Workers Embitter Delta." *New York Times*, July 19, 1964 (excerpts).
http://wihist.org/1u7qew0

RIGHTS WORKERS EMBITTER DELTA

Cleveland, Miss., Defends Negro Status There

By DAVID HALBERSTAM
Special to The New York Times

CLEVELAND, Miss., July 15 —"We have 1 per cent Chinese in this county and we have no Chinese problem. If we had 65 per cent Chinese we might have a Chinese problem."

The speaker was W. B. Alexander Jr., a lawyer and State Senator in this Mississippi Delta city. Cleveland is the county seat of Bolivar County. And in the county—which is typical of the cotton-growing area of Mississippi—two-thirds of the population is neither Chinese nor white, but Negro.

In Cleveland the land is flat and rich. Cotton is the prime crop and accounts for 75 per cent of the county's economy. "Cotton," in the words of Sheriff Charles W. Capps Jr., a planter himself with 2,000 acres, "pays our debts."

The Negro, added Senator Alexander, is "much, much lower than the white man morally." In fact, Mr. Alexander added, "the colored race is a tremendous burden on this state financially and we are bearing it without complaint."

"I believe," Mr. Moore said, "in the right to discriminate by a private person."

As such, virtually all white men in Cleveland oppose the bill, and changes in civil rights are seen as primarily produced by forces outside the South.

"I realize it may sound foolish, but 95 per cent of our blacks are happy. We understand our way of life and we understand each other," said Sheriff Capps.

The local leader of the National Association for the Advancement of Colored People is characterized as an agitator by Mr. Langford. "He' out for personal gain and the local people know it," Mr. Langford said.

Yet, there is concern over some of the changes in the Negro.

"The young Nigras, I am told, are becoming a little more militant. That could create a problem. They are not as respectful, a little more reluctant to say Yessir or No, ma'am," said Mr. Moore.

For this reason there is little sympathy to the white and Negro youths who have entered Bolivar County as part of the summer project.

"To me their motives are unspeakable," said Sheriff Capps. "But I told them I'm going to keep them alive no matter what. We're going to do everything we can to keep the Federal marshals out of Mississippi. Why, just yesterday one of those young people told me that that was their plan—to have the marshals come in to Mississippi.

"They are dirty, they are unclean, they do not dress. The niggers know high-class whites, and no responsible colored people are fooling with them. And yet they come in trying to change this wonderful community of ours," Sheriff Capps said.

Document 2: Residents respond to "Rights Workers Embitter Delta."
http://wihist.org/1yrhrg7
A Freedom Summer volunteer encouraged local Black residents to reply:

In response to your article that was dated July 15, 1964, I want to say that as a negro of Mississippi, I am not happy. The only ones that are happy or think they are happy are the ones that don't know any better, and I don't think I am the only negro that will say this. Some are scared because of the economic situation, meaning that they might lose their jobs, which is only half enough to support their family. The question is, would Sheriff Capps, Governor Paul Johnson or Senator Eastland like to live in my house and send their children to our schools? If so I am sure you would hear a different story.

We're glad that the white people are coming down from the north and that they are thinking of our welfare. Sure we are inferior. The white folks over us every way. They think we ain't nobody. If we had better schools, better books things would be different. If we had better jobs and more money we'd be better off and we'd be more intelligent. We could afford to send our children to school.

Questions

Document 1: "Rights Workers Embitter Delta." *New York Times*, July 19, 1964 (excerpts).

With a partner, agree on answers to these questions. We'll discuss them afterward.

1. Look at the statements by white community leaders in the *New York Times* article. What messages did African Americans get from their political leaders and the other white people quoted? Express their attitude toward their African American neighbors in a single, short sentence of your own.

2. What sorts of people could get their words into the *New York Times*? Who is quoted in that article? What are their jobs and positions? Whose voices are not heard in that article?

3. List three differences between the writing style of Black residents of Bolivar County and the writing style in the first document? Why are they so different?

4. The Black residents who wrote replies did not send them to the *New York Times*. They didn't even sign their names on the copies posted on the local bulletin board. Why not?

Document 3. Cobb, Charles E. "Some Notes on Education" (excerpts).
http://wihist.org/1yrhvfQ

SOME NOTES ON EDUCATION

by Charlie Cobb

What we have discovered over the last few years of our activities
in the South, is that oppression and restriction is not limited
to the bullets of local racists shotgun blasts, or assaults at
county courhouses, or the expulsion of sharecroppers from plantations, but that it (oppression and restriction) is imbeded in a
complex national structure, many of the specifics of which are
oft times difficult to discern, but which govern every facet of
our lives. What is relevant to our lives is constantly defined
for us; we are taught it in every waking hour; it is pounded in
us via radio, T.V., newspapers, etc., most of which are the tools
of our oppressors. Definitions are articulated to us through the
use of terms such as, "qualified", "responsible", "security",
"patriotism", "our way of life", "the american way of life",
"Nigger", "leader", "politics", and a thousand others, infinitely
more subtle and complex. Our lives are pointed out for us in a
millions irrelevant directions, and what we are finding we have
to deal with if we're talking about change (whether in Mississippi
or New York) is, Who points out and determines the direction of
our lives; how do they do it and get away with it ?

Questions

Document 3: Cobb, Charles E. "Some Notes on Education" (excerpts).

With a partner, agree on answers to these questions. We'll discuss them afterward.

1. What's the author's main point in this paragraph? Restate it in your own words.

2. The author says that the things we consider most important—the things we just take for granted—are defined by others. Who was defining those things for kids in Mississippi in 1964? Who does the author say "pounded it into us"?

3. Who puts ideas and information into your mind? Who decides what music gets on the radio, what shows get on television, or what messages get put on billboards and commercials? Who decides what you get to think about, and defines what's normal today? How much money do you suppose they make, compared to a teacher or a worker at McDonalds?

4. In Mississippi in 1964, vicious racism was often considered common sense. List two messages repeated by the media that you consume. What are two things they say are so normal that everyone today thinks they're common sense? How do they encourage you to behave? Who benefits if you do those things?

5. List two things people consider normal today that people 50 years from now might consider weird. Imagine your grandchildren saying, "How could they have thought that?" or "How could they have done that?"

Civil Disobedience

Goals

A classroom activity that separates students by physical characteristics simulates an injustice, which students discuss in light of an excerpt from Martin Luther King's "Letter from a Birmingham Jail" and two segregationist documents. They are challenged to decide what makes a law just or unjust, what makes an action good or bad, and when civil disobedience is acceptable.

Central Questions

Is civil disobedience acceptable? How do you decide when it's OK to break the law? How do you decide if a law is just or unjust? What makes any action right or wrong?

Background Information

Modern thinking about civil disobedience began with the nineteenth-century American author Henry David Thoreau's essay, *Resistance to Civil Government.* In July 1846, Thoreau went to jail for refusing to pay taxes to a government that supported slavery. Tolstoy, Gandhi, and Martin Luther King, Jr. all read Thoreau's essay and extended his ideas by promoting nonviolent civil disobedience as a means to social change.

Both Gandhi and King argued against responding to violence with more violence. They also believed that those who practice nonviolence occupy a moral high ground compared to their oppressors. Like Thoreau, Gandhi and King believed that individuals have a moral responsibility to disobey a law if it is unjust. But how do we decide if a law is unjust?

The two most common ways for deciding are called natural rights and utilitarianism.

Believers in natural rights argue that there are universal laws more powerful than any government, and we discover them through our conscience or our religious faith. From this perspective, a good action is one that harmonizes with our inner sense of morality. It's based on feelings.

Believers in utilitarianism argue that a good action is one that helps the greatest number of people or produces the least amount of suffering. From this viewpoint, a good action is one that produces clear benefits in the world. It's based on reasoning.

Both approaches have problems. A person listening only to their conscience might be mistaken or confused—suicide bombers obey what they believe in their hearts is a higher law. But a person trying to be utilitarian has to try to predict the future consequences of their action, and they can easily be wrong: even Stalin and Hitler believed that their actions would create more happiness than suffering.

Documents Used in This Lesson:

1. Examples of Jim Crow laws from Mississippi.
   http://wihist.org/1w1Ab2d

2. Example of a flawed justice system, Pike County, Mississippi, October 1964. From, "Mississippi: The Long Winter Ahead" in NAACP Legal Defense and Education Fund report, vol. II, no. 2 (Oct.-Nov.1964)
   http://wihist.org/1Bqrz9P

3. King, Martin Luther, "Letter from a Birmingham Jail" (excerpt). http://wihist.org/15X9d3r

Civil Disobedience: Activities

(Activities to be used with both pages of documents.)

Without telling students why, ask them to gather all their belongings and stand up. Direct all blue-eyed students (or red-haired, or left-handed, etc.) to take seats at the back of the room and the others to sit at the front.

Instruct students at the front to listen to music on headphones, read for pleasure, or enjoy some other quiet pleasure.

Tell the group in the back that they're having a pop quiz worth ten per cent of their grade for the term. Insist that the quiz be completed in pencil or red ink or some other arbitrary way that will exclude some of the group, and that people who don't obey this rule will receive no credit at all.

Keep discriminating between the two groups—give treats to those in front, impose an unrealistic time limit on those in back, etc.—until some students in the back object or refuse to participate. Then direct students to return to their usual seats and discuss what happened:

1. Ask one or more of the protesters to explain how they felt.

2. Ask everyone whether the rules were fair.

3. How did they know the rules were unfair? What makes a rule fair?

4. Ask the protesters why they refused to obey. Distinguish emotion/personal displeasure from principle as a motive for civil disobedience.

5. Hand out the sheet with Jim Crow laws. Ask everyone if they would have obeyed or broken those laws if they lived in the South in the 1960s. Why?

6. Direct their attention to Document 2 on the same sheet. What do you think happened to civil rights workers who appeared in that courtroom? How could that situation be remedied so justice could be served in the local courts?

7. What makes a law unjust? (*Try to tease out the natural rights and utilitarian arguments. Define them on the blackboard, from the first page of this lesson plan.*)

8. Hand out Document 3, Martin Luther King's explanation, and the questions based on it; complete in pairs, and discuss.

9. Ask them to work in small groups and reach consensus on how to resolve the following ethical dilemma:

Your friend Alex has been dating Terry for weeks, and Alex thinks it's a long-term monogamous relationship. You're surprised, then, to notice Terry making out at the mall with your other old friend, Cassidy, who goes to a different school. As you leave the bus together, Cassidy tells you they've been dating for a month and are really in love. Do you tell Alex about the disloyalty, or tell Cassidy? Do you say nothing at all?

Document 1: Examples of Jim Crow laws from Mississippi.

Here are three state laws that were enforced by police in Mississippi. Other laws passed by counties and cities segregated the races even more and gave police power to arrest and punish people who disobeyed them.

a. "Separate free schools shall be established for the education of children of African descent; and it shall be unlawful for any colored child to attend any white school, or any white child to attend a colored school."

b. "The marriage of a white person with a negro or mulatto or person who shall have one-eighth or more of negro blood shall be unlawful and void."

c. "Any person guilty of printing, publishing or circulating matter urging or presenting arguments in favor of social equality or of intermarriage between whites and negroes, shall be guilty of a misdemeanor."

Document 2: Example of a flawed justice system (Pike County, Mississippi, October 1964).
This article describes the trial of nine white men in McComb, Mississippi, who admitted to bombing the homes of Black residents working for civil rights.

> on October 23 Pike County Circuit Judge W. H. Watkins gave suspended sentences to nine white men (from "good families") convicted of bombing three Negro homes. He also placed the nine, some of whom faced possible death penalties for illegally using explosives, on probation. Some of them had pleaded guilty, while the others entered pleas of "no contest."
>
> In a 30-minute lecture, Judge Watkins told the nine that the civil rights workers in McComb had "unduly provoked" them. "Their presence here was unnerving and unwanted," the Judge continued. "Some of them are people of low morality and unhygienic."
>
> The Judge further said he was suspending their sentences because "You are mostly young men (four are over 35, one is 44) starting out and you apparently deserve a second chance."

Document 3: King, Martin Luther, "Letter from a Birmingham Jail" (excerpt). In 1963, Dr. King wrote a letter to other ministers to explain why he broke the law and went to jail.
http://wihist.org/15X9d3r

You express a great deal of anxiety over our willingness to break laws. This is certainly a legitimate concern. Since we so diligently urge people to obey the Supreme Court's decision of 1954 outlawing segregation in the public schools, it is rather strange and paradoxical to find us consciously breaking laws. One may well ask, "How can you advocate breaking some laws and obeying others?" The answer is found in the fact that there are two types of laws: There are just laws and there are unjust laws. I would be the first to advocate obeying just laws. One has not only a legal but moral responsibility to obey just laws. Conversely, one has a moral responsibility to disobey unjust laws. I would agree

with Saint Augustine that "An unjust law is no law at all."

Now what is the difference between the two? How does one determine when a law is just or unjust? A just law is a man-made code that squares with the moral law or the law of God. An unjust law is a code that is out of harmony with the moral law. To put it in the terms of Saint Thomas Aquinas, an unjust law is a human law that is not rooted in eternal and natural law. Any law that uplifts human personality is just. Any law that degrades human personality is unjust. All segregation statutes are unjust because segregation distorts the soul and damages the personality. It gives the segregator a false sense of superiority and the segregated a false sense of inferiority. To use the words of Martin Buber, the great Jewish philosopher, segregation substitutes an "I-it" relationship for the "I-thou" relationship, and ends up relegating persons to the status of things. So segregation is not only politically, economically, and sociologically unsound, but it is morally wrong and sinful. Paul Tillich has said that sin is separation. Isn't segregation an existential expression of man's tragic separation, an expression of his awful estrangement, his terrible sinfulness? So I can urge men to obey the 1954 decision of the Supreme Court because it is morally right, and I can urge them to disobey segregation ordinances because they are morally wrong....

Questions

Document 3: King, Martin Luther, "Letter from a Birmingham Jail" (excerpt).

Work with a partner to read the two paragraphs and agree on answers to these questions.

1. Why does Dr. King think it's okay to break the law sometimes? In fact, he says it's our moral obligation to sometimes break the law. When?

2. What does he think makes a law just? What makes a law unjust, in his opinion? Express what he means in a single sentence of your own.

3. But racists thought they were being moral, too, and for the same reasons as Dr. King. Here's a quote from a pamphlet published the same year as his letter by opponents of the Civil Rights Movement:
    "The races of man are the handiwork of God, as is everything in nature. If He had wanted only one type of man, He would have created only one. The Holy Bible does not advocate integration. In fact, it advocates racial separation." (Citizen's Council. *Racial Facts* (Greenwood, Miss., May 1964). http://tinyurl.com/mtlpjss
    Why do you agree with Dr. King instead of the other pamphlet? Give two reasons, in your own words.

Correlation of Lessons with Professional Standards

Concise summary	Standard	Lesson 1	Lesson 2	Lesson 3	Lesson 4	Lesson 5	Lesson 6	Lesson 7	Lesson 8	Lesson 9	Lesson 10
Determine a central idea & analyze it	MPS-R8.2		×	×	×	×	×	×	×	×	×
Determine an author's point of view or purpose	MPS-R8.6		×	×	×	×	×	×	×	×	×
Delineate & evaluate an argument & claims	MPS-R8.8			×				×			
Analyze two or more texts that conflict	MPS-R8.9						×				
Write informative texts to convey ideas	MPS-L8.2	×			×	×					
Write narratives using well-structured sequences	MPS-L8.3				×	×					
Draw evidence to support analysis, reflection	MPS-L8.9	×	×	×	×	×	×	×	×	×	×
History: use a variety of resources to interpret events	DPI-H8	×	×	×	×	×	×	×	×	×	×
Civics: study uses of power, authority, & governance	DPI-C8		×		×	×	×	×	×	×	×
Economics: production, exchange, & consumption	DPI-E8					×			×		
Determine central ideas of a text & analyze them	CC-RI.11-12.2		×	×	×	×	×	×	×	×	×
Determine an author's point of view or purpose	CC-RI.11-12.6		×	×			×	×			×
Integrate & evaluate multiple sources of information	CC-RI.11-12.7	×	×	×	×	×	×	×	×	×	×
Write arguments to support claims	CC-W.11-12.1	×	×	×	×	×					
Write texts to examine & convey complex ideas	CC-W.11-12.2		×	×	×	×				×	
Write narratives using well-structured event sequences	CC-W.11-12.3			×	×	×					
Determine central idea; provide accurate summary	CC-H.11-12.2		×	×	×	×	×	×	×	×	×
Evaluate explanations, correlate with evidence	CC-H.11-12.3	×						×			
Analyze how a complex primary source is structured	CC-H.11-12.5		×	×	×	×					
Evaluate differing points of view on same event	CC-H.11-12.6							×			
Evaluate multiple sources in diverse formats	CC-H.11-12.7	×	×	×	×	×	×	×	×	×	×
Evaluate an author's premises, claims, & evidence	CC-H.11-12.8							×	×		
Integrate information from diverse sources	CC-H.11-12.9	×	×	×	×	×	×	×	×	×	×

Concise summary	Standard	Lesson 11	Lesson 12	Lesson 13	Lesson 14	Lesson 15	Lesson 16	Lesson 17	Lesson 18	Lesson 19	Lesson 20
Determine a central idea & analyze it	MPS-R8.2	X	X	X	X	X	X	X	X	X	X
Determine an author's point of view or purpose	MPS-R8.6	X	X	X	X	X	X		X	X	X
Delineate & evaluate an argument & claims	MPS-R8.8	X			X				X	X	X
Analyze two or more texts that conflict	MPS-R8.9	X			X	X	X		X	X	X
Write informative texts to convey ideas	MPS-L8.2			X		X		X			
Write narratives using well-structured sequences	MPS-L8.3	X	X	X							
Draw evidence to support analysis, reflection	MPS-L8.9	X	X	X	X	X	X	X	X	X	X
History: use a variety of resources to interpret events	DPI-H8	X	X	X	X	X	X	X	X	X	X
Civics: study uses of power, authority, & governance	DPI-C8	X	X		X	X	X	X	X	X	X
Economics: production, exchange, & consumption	DPI-E8	X		X			X			X	
Determine central ideas of a text & analyze them	CC-RI.11-12.2	X	X	X	X	X	X	X	X	X	X
Determine an author's point of view or purpose	CC-RI.11-12.6	X	X	X	X	X	X	X	X	X	X
Integrate & evaluate multiple sources of information	CC-RI.11-12.7	X	X	X	X	X	X	X	X	X	X
Write arguments to support claims	CC-W.11-12.1	X						X			
Write texts to examine & convey complex ideas	CC-W.11-12.2			X				X			
Write narratives using well-structured event sequences	CC-W.11-12.3		X	X							
Determine central idea; provide accurate summary	CC-H.11-12.2	X	X	X	X	X	X	X	X	X	X
Evaluate explanations, correlate with evidence	CC-H.11-12.3	X			X	X	X			X	X
Analyze how a complex primary source is structured	CC-H.11-12.5	X	X			X			X		X
Evaluate differing points of view on same event	CC-H.11-12.6	X		X	X			X	X	X	X
Evaluate multiple sources in diverse formats	CC-H.11-12.7	X	X	X	X	X	X	X	X	X	X
Evaluate an author's premises, claims, & evidence	CC-H.11-12.8	X			X			X	X	X	X
Integrate information from diverse sources	CC-H.11-12.9	X	X	X	X	X	X	X	X	X	X

MPS = Milwaukee Public Schools   DPO = Wisconsin Department of Public Instruction   CC = Common Core